gretchen schauffler

D0932770

devine

Color

when color sings

INKWATER
PRESS

Portland · Oregon

Dedication

I DEDICATE THIS BOOK to those who know what it is to hear perfection sing and those who long for it. Somewhere between a high soaring pitch and a low vibrating hum, you hear it the minute you see it, taste it, or feel it. It is what you hear the moment you know something is the best it can be and you wouldn't want it any other way. It is a song so sweet and satisfying it makes you dance to a happy beat regardless of who is watching. You have no need to explain it, rationalize it, or justify it. You no longer need hear from anyone else it is good because you know it is.

This is for those of you who want to hear color sing!

Table of Contents

Acknowledgments

THANK GOD, I REALLY...REALLY thank God. He saw over every opportunity, missed opportunity, understanding, misunderstanding, person, place, time, pursuit, and surrender to make Devine Color a philosophy that transforms the lives of those who want to live in their color imagination.

To my husband, Scott, my soul mate, who listens to everything I have to say over and over again and always does it with a smile because one of the things he loves about me is my voice (good thing).

To my incredible kids: Lily, Mia, Max, and Griffin, the greatest gift of my life was having you girls and the icing on my cake was getting you boys! You make planet earth my heaven.

To my mother and grandmother, the "Ana's" who always thought I took a path that was a little different than they believed I should take but in the end, they had faith it would lead to "greatness." (They prayed a lot.)

To my business partners, business associates, and business co-workers who sometimes do not know what I am talking about when I always take a path that is a little different than they think I should take yet trust in the end it will lead to "great." (They are a lot like the "Ana's.")

To my alter-universe twin, Jody (just Jody), who is my "Edna Mode," always reminding me I am "Elast-a-girl."

To my bouquet of friends whom I love and depend on, who cheer, cry, laugh, drink (some more than others), and fight with me every step of the way towards this life. You know who you are because you have my cell number and do not mind that I swear.

To all my clients, especially the first ones (you know who you are) who really took a chance on me and believed me when I said, "These colors will sing to you."

To those in the paint industry who embraced me (some hugged tighter than others) and blazed a path to make and sell paint that goes on like yogurt and looks like chiffon, even though they didn't know what chiffon was.

To my color consultants who bring their experience, passion, and insights every day to a home and leave it at the front door so color can become perfectly meaningful to someone else...I thank you and my clients thank you! For the many PFC's I personally thank you.

To the painters who were confident, optimistic, and open-minded when they decided to try Devine Color, a paint line they had never heard of, by some artist they had never heard of, with names (not numbers) that were hard to pronounce like Merlot, Shiraz, and Toile and despite the vocabulary hurdles, recommended it to their clients as perfect colors that actually had perfect paint to go with them.

To my childhood island of Puerto Rico, where the lesson is that you can never dance enough, sing enough, laugh enough, or have enough color.

To the great Northwest whose mild, rich, green and gray winters, purple mountains, pumpkin deserts, wild Coast Range and glorious summers display the awesome beauty of nature and the ideal place to let your imagination take over, creating a lifestyle that offers the perfect cup of coffee, spiritual teas, fast running shoes, outdoor couture, nerdy technology, woolen blankets, organic chocolate, pinot everything, ground-breaking music, and of course, perfect color.

Introduction

WHY WOULD I WANT to write a book about color when there are so many great books out there with beautiful pictures, charts, combinations, explanations, and observations? Almost everything has been said. *Almost* is where I come in. I encourage you to read as much as you can about color theory and look for color ideas, but when you're ready to go further, this book is about the *almost* part that is generally not discussed.

It is not what you know about color but the way you see it and feel it that makes its meaning important, because beautiful colors together resonate with your psyche and feed your soul. You were born to receive this gift. Here is how this gift works. You have eyes that allow you to see, but color enables you to understand the world around you. Color is a constant that is channeled through your eyes and into your brain. You are then able to translate that information into an understanding of beauty.

When we see color in perfect relationships, we all understand the experience. Nature teaches us that color relationships are meant to be in beautiful combinations that we can all understand. It is called beauty.

You can instantly recognize when perfect colors sing. When you see a sunset from your dining room window blazing in or look at the rich, deep, endless blues in the ocean or get lost in the details of color splashes on a canvas, you become enraptured. It's almost a moment of transcendence, when you're not just seeing individual objects, but feeling the fullness of life. That is the connection that color brings, one that gives you instant peace.

I know what it is to see and feel color outside, but what I want is to change your mind about how you see color inside your home so you can begin to feel the same mesmerizing magic of color relationships. Your indoor world is just as important as the outdoors and the same color combinations are possible.

This is probably one of the few times a book has been written about color essentially in black and white. I couldn't think of a better way to talk about the way we see color without the distraction of color images. And this is what we need to do, talk about color so we can start changing our minds about how to see it.

By the time you finish this book, you will have developed a greater understanding of how you see color and how to put colors together so that your world rocks you as much as when you see a perfect sunset. I believe that making those changes will bring the things you love into focus by allowing everything — the colors in your new furniture, old furniture, brickwork, appliances, tile, rugs, woodwork, and especially your artwork and collections — to work together perfectly.

At the end of this book I have a reference to my "color web peeks" at www.devinecolor.com/colorpeeks/ where you'll be able to experience the concepts I've discussed. When you go to the site you will be able to gaze upon gorgeous pictures of different color relationships, most of them taken from our natural world. These pictures represent the six colors of the rainbow giving us the best nature has to offer. But first, let's start talking about color in plain black and white.

devine color

when color sings

The Truth
Behind What We Experience

In a Perfect World . . .

THEY SAY THE DEFINITION of insanity is to do the same thing over and over again expecting a different result. We live in a world full of things we can't change or won't change and some things we have more control over. How we go about change keeps us preoccupied and takes up a big chunk of our lives. The one thing for certain is that no matter how complicated this world gets, there is always the undeniable beauty of nature and its perfect color. Color is one of the elements in our lives that can change our perceptions of reality.

The phrase, "Well, in a perfect world..." implies that the world is not perfect. Since I don't have a clear vision of what this perfect world is, I can only tell you about what *my* perfect world would look like. I would want to be in

> Who in the rainbow can draw the line where the violet tint ends and the orange tint begins? Distinctly we see the difference of the colors, but where exactly does the one first blendingly enter into the other? So with sanity and insanity.
>
> ~ Herman Melville

charge of everything and everyone would think like I do. Somehow I don't think this would be exactly perfect for other people. This is what makes the world so challenging for us! We all have our own versions of perfection.

True, while we are at the mercy of nature, relationships, opportunities, circumstances, information, education, economy, and the universal forces that control us everyday, no matter what, our daily journey always ends at the front door of our homes. When we walk in and leave the bigger world behind, we enter a personal sanctuary where we have gathered our belongings and created our own small world — a world we share with our loved ones, our families, and our neighbors. This is the world I want to talk about.

The gift of nature with its perfect color provides us with immeasurable pleasure and gives this world of ours the spoonful of sugar that makes the medicine go down, so to speak. Nature has already taught us it can be done. Nothing is more flexible and forgiving of change than the splendor of color outdoors — the changing seasons, the moods of the sky, the individual personalities of plants and flowers. This is what I believe in — color can make relationships between all things, making them appear perfect, no matter how new or old.

My knack for making perfect color has to do with making color relationships out of what people own and that means having to really look at what is there. How hard is this? Well, everything in our homes tells a tale of love, hate, beauty, history, worship, neglect, or regret. It's that change thing. You have things that can and can't change. It's an emotional, confusing, and very personal task.

Having people explain how they feel about their possessions tells a lot about how they feel about their lives. Regardless of what they have to say, I always bring to light the one true resource they have in front of them to make their home what they want it to be. Color. Color is what turns their life inventory into absolute, pure, unadulterated pleasure. If you look at your belongings as beautiful as well as purposeful, you accomplish two things, a reason for them to be part of your life and a reason to love them. You can then think of them without apologies, regrets, needs, or wants — just beauty.

I want to leave everyone crazy in love with what they see and not with what they own.

Just as we view the beauties of nature, I want to leave everyone crazy in love with what they see and not with what they own. In nature, when your eyes are so busy loving all the colors, you think of them as one big color palette. Color does not live in isolation, so it can't be about a decayed color on a shrub or an extraordinary color on a flower. How color in nature gets to be perfect is through an illusion of color relationships that lets your mind rest and gaze upon a world where you wouldn't want to change a thing.

What if you felt you didn't have to change a thing? How would you feel if you lived with a perfect combination of colors that made your home stunning? Well, we are about to find out. By the time you finish this book I would like you to believe in one thing: when perfect color sings, it is going to make the difference between what you can live with and what you cannot.

When perfect color sings, it is going to make the difference between what you can live with and what you cannot.

Inside our homes we all seem to have some major unfinished business. We have couches with colors we like along with ugly tile we hate in the bathroom. There are things that have reason, but also things that have no rhyme. Believe it or not, that is exactly how nature is. Even the most pristine mountain or rough coastline has undesirable colors, yet is stunning to see. Why not combine stunning color with your old carpet?

The more "behind closed doors" I was let into, the more I found people apologizing for what they had. So many times I kept hearing comments such as, Well, don't look at that because it's not going to be there next year, or Ignore the couch because we hate it, and the one that surprised me to no end: I'm not attached to anything! How did people end up with all this stuff and not care about half of it?

So let's talk about homes that are all coordinated, where everything matches. Their owners have endless design talent and resources, extra time, and most of all, money. It's enough to make anyone jealous. It shouldn't. That twinge of envy comes from most of us believing that those people live in a perfect world. Things appear to be done, finished, and there is no need to change. So when we hear about a divorce, or their kids doing drugs, we are shocked because that is not how perfection behaves. In a perfect world, things should be as perfect as they look.

Whether a 5,000-square-foot home with brand-new furniture or a three-bedroom ranch with old furniture, homes are the means by which we meet our needs to cook, sleep, sit, and read, as well as nurture ourselves and our families. Everyone has a love-hate relationship with what they

> Artists can color the sky red because they know it's blue. Those of us who aren't artists must color things the way they really are or people might think we're stupid.
>
> ~ Jules Feiffer

Everyone has a love-hate relationship with what they own, and this book is about finding joy and beauty in the midst of constant change.

own, and this book is about finding joy and beauty in the midst of constant change. I gained a lot of practice at injecting color harmony and excitement into homes and neighborhoods where the up-and-coming executives came and went while building their careers.

Nothing says change like the corporate ladder, but there are many levels and types of ladders in people's lives. We live in a world where everyone seems to want to climb upward to feel like they are on the road to somewhere. And of course, this means change and forward movement can make you absolutely dizzy if you're not careful.

Corporations have a way of keeping their employees moving and shaking with company transfers. I was hired a lot by couples in these transitional times, since I have a way of helping these families stay grounded. Their homes were neutral-colored houses in neighborhoods known as "transfer row." Companies transferred their new employees to town and these were great places for them to land while they waited to be transferred again to bigger and better opportunities.

Everyone was on the same path: one career, one homemaker, 2.5 kids, and a pet of choice. They had neighborhood regulations that included landscaping restrictions along with an exterior color committee to make sure your color was not offensive. It was as perfect a world as you could live in considering the working world of the corporate ladder.

I received a call from one such client who was ready to set down some roots while waiting around to see where she and her family would end up next. She was ready to make a change and create a new environment inside her own front door.

As always I had to talk about what we could or could not change, otherwise known as the "right now." With everyone having a foot in the future, it was really hard to say to them, "I'd rather you have one year of perfect beauty through color than ten years of waiting to live a perfect life!" We knew the colors in her woodwork, tiles, and other permanent surfaces were not going to change and therefore they would have to become part of the color palette.

But what about the things that were subject to change and weren't nailed down to the floor? Whenever I talked about including the colors of her couches, chairs, or accessories sprinkled throughout the house, she asked me to ignore them, or to overlook them. These were all a reminder of how many times she had replaced her furniture to fit the new environment, or how many times she had packed

> I'd rather you have one year of perfect beauty through color than ten years of waiting to live a perfect life!

the same things that now looked like misfits in this newest house. Everything was functional, most of it completely impersonal.

So I walked over to a small art piece on a huge wall looking all lonely and said, "I love this, it's perfect. Let's bring it into the mix!" She looked astonished and almost embarrassed. I couldn't tell what she was thinking, but I knew this was beautiful and personal to her.

This was the only thing she had kept from a time when she was single, before she had kids and had settled in "transfer row." She had given up on this little glimpse of herself. She couldn't believe she had ignored all those amazing colors swirled in that small piece of art. Those colors had sung to her long ago and the song was loud and clear again. This piece was not perfect, or important, but the colors made it beautiful. That beauty was undeniable to her when she first purchased it and to me when I saw it. That is what I mean when I say that perfect color sings.

I pointed out that, among all the impersonal things, it seemed like a world that was so bright and exciting, but regrettably the total opposite mood of her home. We had to get her out of the "regret" mode right away.

So why do we regret? It is always something we should have done, could have done, or didn't do. In other words, were there things left to do in this woman's life that were on hold? I don't know, but what I did know was that taking the colors in that art piece and helping her live out loud with them would make her feel like she was in the moment, as a matter of fact, in *her* moment. Isn't a perfect world one that does not need to change, at least for right now?

We took those colors and built her whole house around them. The first thing was to find out which color had the most in common with all the colors existing in the home. Then we created combinations with these colors that looked beautiful, and finally placed them where they belonged. All the other existing colors in the home surrendered to her color palette, becoming transformed into her own version of perfect beauty, inside the less-than-perfect world of her perfect neighborhood.

Your Turn

Take a moment right now and choose one thing (if there are many, be selective by taking the most colorful ones) from each room in your home that you absolutely love to look at or that has a deep connection to your past. Make a pile of them in front of you. Name the colors out loud. There are differing shapes and textures, but most of all, it's all about color! These are the colors your eyes love to feel and the colors that have followed you throughout your life changes.

This is what this book will show you: how to see the magic of color in everything you own and how to make relationships out of color that will make it all look beautiful and personal. Most of all, you will hear it sing.

Color Is Not About One Person's Opinion — It's About a Shared Experience

IN MOST CITIES, THERE is a cluster of model homes featured by high-end builders with the latest products and local craftsmanship. In Portland, Oregon, it's an annual show called the Street of Dreams which takes place at a top-of-the-hill, crème-de-la-crème neighborhood. The general public gets to tour the homes knowing few can afford them, but at least they can take home an image of what perfect would be if you could wrap it up and take it home.

Luckily, I got hooked up with a very well known designer who, at that time, was a local celebrity and had a reputation for being a visionary. Everyone felt he knew where he was going with his vision and I was going to follow him straight to the

> The little may contrast with the great, in painting, but cannot be said to be contrary to it. Oppositions of colors contrast; but there are also colors contrary to each other, that is, which produce an ill effect because they shock the eye when brought very near it.
>
> ~ Voltaire

guest powder bath in his project at the Street of Dreams. I was so ready for the challenge!

My color work was going to be seen by everyone. Then came the one of several turning points that took me from being a color consultant to being a color philosopher. He hated my perfect colors!

I had mixed rich greens and burnt terracotta shades to make the walls look like they had aged to a green perfection. This was a perfect color collection, or so I thought, with the orange terracotta tiles in the bathroom and the greens woven throughout the orange, burnt red, and sage green fabrics in the living room.

At first he found them to be "too bright" and I quickly realized that a bit more muting would bring the walls back a bit. Better? No, he wanted them *way* back. I tried several times to make the color look the way he wanted, but he kept asking if I could change it.

If I couldn't show one person the beauty of color, how could I show many? So I graciously resigned from the position of powder room color queen and realized that the problem was the fact that beauty was in the eye of the beholder, the beholder in this case being a designer who had differing ideas.

Everyone's eyes are equipped to recognize beautiful color combinations but recreating the "feeling" of what we see is another story. There are limitations to color and this is what I'll be helping you to recognize. One way is to understand that not every color can be used just anywhere or combined with just any other color. And like colors in a great painting, perfect color does not stand alone. It is the connection, relationship, and position of a color in an environment that makes it perfect. When it is perfect, everyone can recognize it regardless of how much education, understanding, or color experience they have. Look outside the box literally; look outside to nature.

And like colors in a great painting, perfect color does not stand alone. It is the connection, relationship, and position of a color in an environment that makes it perfect.

You can hate the color orange and yet look at a sunset and find it necessary among all the other colors to see perfection. As a matter of fact, you would never take it out. You are not asking why it is there or if it makes sense; you love it instantly with your eyes. Because of the perfect combination of colors, the person next to you will feel the same way. Color, while personal, is not private.

Every color wants to be in a great combination, everyone wants the combinations to be great, and everyone wants to see perfect color. Our eyes are wired to see thousands of color combinations in nature and our brains enjoy them as perfect. We inherently want this kind of pleasure with everything that crosses our line of sight.

When anyone arrives at the Street of Dreams or any other private world they walk into, they bring along their color opinions based on their own personal experiences — rules, fears, opinions, trends, judgments, biases, and loves or hates that shape their views and influence their choices. *"You can't put that color with that one"* or *"That's too much color"* are some of the comments that spread like wildfire and diminish our confidence, yet end up on the tip of our tongues ready to be spit out the next time someone else attempts to do something with color.

These collective opinions leave us feeling confused as to what we actually know about color and who the real experts are. The expert part is complicated because, while color is part physics and biology, it is also part art and creativity. One explains the science of light and vision while the other feeds the expression of the human soul.

...while color is part physics and biology, it is also part art and creativity. One explains the science of light and vision while the other feeds the expression of the human soul.

We all have to learn about the science of color to fundamentally understand our world and even our language. Yet once you leave the classroom and the books close, that is the end of the black-and-white discussion of color as a science.

That's when the gray talk begins. We talk about colors we love or hate, would like to or can't have. We talk about how we feel and react to the colors around us because it is not about what we know anymore, it is about what we want: the great feeling we get from colors when we see something perfectly beautiful.

This book does not talk about expertise or what we think we already believe. It is about changing your mind about how you see color and how perfect color, as in nature, can make your personal world full of beauty that everyone can recognize. It is a life-affirming experience, especially when it is shared.

It talks about all the things we say and think about color that become rules and the truth behind what we see and how we experience it. But most of all, this book

Most of all, this book is about empowering your life with the colors you love, so that every time you walk in through your front door, you are not focusing on what you will change or want to change, you will just see something that takes your breath away.

is about empowering your life with the colors you love, so that every time you walk in through your front door, you are not focusing on what you will change or want to change, you will just see something that takes your breath away.

Your Turn

Take a public place and a private place and compare what you see. Next time you walk into a restaurant, hotel, or a friend's home that is beautiful in your mind but not to your personal taste, ask yourself how the color impacts the space. What colors are present and how does that beauty make you feel? Does the Italian restaurant where you love to have dinner give you a different feeling than the French cottage home of a friend you love to visit? What are the differences in the color relationships between those two places?

Can you think of homes or restaurants you don't like? Try to remember those colors and think about the feeling you get from them.

Why I Need Colors to Sing and So Do You

TALK ABOUT THINGS YOU can't change! When I was ten, my mother moved from one end of the world to another. It would be years before I could accept this reality. She had moved from San Juan, a very metro Caribbean city in Puerto Rico, to a country setting in Hillsboro, Oregon. Nothing was the same. It was a decade before I could permanently move to Portland and finish college. Going back and forth between the cultures gave me a lot of insight as to how things were really never perfect. It was all in how you looked at it.

> Color possesses me. I don't have to pursue it. It will possess me always, I know it. This is the meaning of this happy hour: color and I are one, I am a painter.
>
> ~ Paul Klee

In college, I started to major in Art Therapy but I realized I would only have that kind of patience for my own kids. I switched to Architecture but hated math and straight lines. Thinking more along freeform lines, I switched to Fashion Design only to find myself doing math again, only with scissors. So I settled for Graphic Design, got a BA, and went straight to work in sales.

Suburbia is where I found myself walking into my front door after I quit my career in pharmaceutical sales and started making babies. It was the early nineties. Demi Moore, Maria Shriver, and Kathie Lee Gifford were also birthing away. It was nesting time and Martha Stewart had just started to build her home engineering empire and *Sunset Magazine* was the NW lifestyle bible. Couples moved into these sprawling subdivisions to build safe futures for their families and to create their own personal worlds.

How personal were these worlds? Think of how many lifestyle changes people go through. Think about how someone goes from living in a dorm and having roommates, to living in an apartment, getting a job, buying a house, or living in a condo. How about being single, married, single, married, and single again? Or yes, what about the good old "we are only going to have two kids" when the third one shows up after you had attended the last kindergarten graduation?

For many in suburbia, long gone were the frat parties, sorority sing-a-longs, and late-night clubbing. In were the wedding and baby showers, outdoor grilling parties, margarita mixes, and computer games. The suburbs represented family, faith, real estate, good schools — in other words, a sense of community. This communal approach was a perfect breeding ground for color experts and opinions to flourish.

Color conversations among us were more like hearsay — the kind of hearsay that always makes you feel like you only have part of the story. We all came from different backgrounds and education regarding the rules of color. We tried to keep up with the latest magazines and forecasts; still so many questions with no clear answers. *"Are there too many colors because I can't find the right one?" "What do you mean my old blue couch is no longer in; I heard blue is coming back? Do I wait for it to come back?" "You can't do that color with that one!"* The questions and opinions never stopped.

Was my yellow mellow enough? Was her tile too pink? Were my walls too red? No, yes, maybe. Everyone had an opinion. Just when you thought you had it figured out, the next person gave you a different story, or worse, made you think there was only one answer, *hers*.

It was when I quit my job and nestled in suburbia that I found myself embracing the artistic me again. I found a way to experiment with a collage technique that helped me create color compositions with anything — from solid and printed papers to textures and paint. This became the ground-work for my understanding of color relationships that later on became my signature as a color consultant.

What stood out about my style was the way my color relationships worked. They were complex, yet easy on the eye, and they instantly let you understand and feel them.

Growing up in Puerto Rico I lived with boundless color. Color is timeless in the Caribbean and it's a place where buildings are hot pink, orange, yellow, ocean blue, and parrot green. Because it's a destination nestled between America and Europe, both influenced the styles and colors of the culture. It was easy to love both the old and the new. This is the color baggage I brought with me to my world and I was not afraid of it. Quite the contrary!

Wanting to create backgrounds for my art I began working on colors for my home. I was always looking for reds that were more coral, greens with more yellow, and blues that were greener. These were not anywhere to be found. As a matter of fact, you couldn't even find colors to go with them. It was the era of hunter green and jewel tones. No celery, avocado, chartreuse, lime, mango, or kiwi available. So, you found me at yard sales, hoping to come across that old avocado green party tray or a 1950s flamingo pattern that I could take home and make mine. Then I would mix colors to go with them.

Painting was my vehicle for making color experiments inside during the rainy winter months of the Northwest and what allowed me to recreate the warm Puerto Rican climate for my home. The magic combination was finding the colors I loved, making colors to go with them, and combining them with the things that couldn't change.

Everyone who came to my home seemed to love looking at the colors that expressed my feelings and personality. Everything looked like it all belonged. The colors worked so well together that people could hear the music and the song was contagious. That's what everyone wanted for himself or herself — not using precisely the same colors — but achieving that same feeling for their homes.

These colors were designed to be the connectors, the missing links between the things you already owned and those you would acquire later on.

The northwest corner of the United States is synonymous with nature. It is no surprise that from mountains, to oceans, to rivers and deserts, this part of the country turns nature into a lifestyle. As an artist

I realized that the perfect colors of nature in the Caribbean or in the Northwest never changed. By bringing these colors into my home I could live my life, not with my feet in the past or the future, but firmly planted in the "now."

The word got out about my color consulting and my color philosophy. I worked with a regional paint company and together we developed a color paint line that delivered perfect color in gallons of paint that went on like yogurt and looked like chiffon. These colors were designed to be the connectors, the missing links between the things you already owned and those you would acquire later on. Some didn't even know what chiffon was and didn't care; it was 40 yards of color that made the world a better place. Devine Color became "Color Therapy from the Northwest," a trend-proof color line as seen in nature.

When Devine Color was launched in Ireland, the colors that were developed inside a garage in an American suburban home became integral colors with 400-year-old tapestries, antiques, and modern art pieces. That's what I would call ageless.

My philosophy, like color television, is all there in black and white.

~ from Monty Python's *Flying Circus*

Your Turn

Track your own life's journey through color. Think of the colors that surrounded you when you were a kid — in your home, your closet, or your climate. Think about favorite toys, dresses or shoes, wall colors, or art. Bring up the memories. Think where you are now and see if you can make a timetable to track the colors that impacted you the most.

In my timetable, I remember white walls and a white house; my grandmother's blue-green couch; charcoal tables; lime green jewels; a pink-and-white bedroom (my mother's idea); our blue toilet; coral, light green, and white dresses; white go-go boots; white maternity dress; coral marble fireplace with coral walls; cream lacquered tables and a cream leather set; and a charcoal carpet.

The Truth
Behind What We Think

"THERE ARE TOO MANY COLORS"

THERE ARE ONLY SIX
(OK, there are really seven but two are purple)

ASK ANYONE WHAT COLOR they want, and they give you a fantasy. They want an oasis blue like a dark, deep pond in the middle of the desert. They want a bright, sunny, warm yellow like a ray right out of a sunburst. They want a cool, warm moss green like the fur on a tree trunk in a shady spot. They want to feel the coals burning from a red that smolders.

OK, so they haven't been to an oasis in the middle of the desert or really want to feel the burning coals, but the imagination is a great place to live if you are looking for the magic of color. There are thousands of ways to get there. Every time we look outside there are so many different versions of colors that the number is constantly changing. Some say 10,000, some 20,000. The fact is when you consider

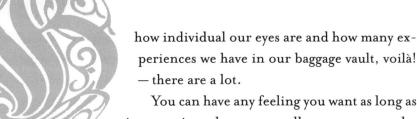

how individual our eyes are and how many experiences we have in our baggage vault, voilà! — there are a lot.

You can have any feeling you want as long as it comes in red, orange, yellow, green, purple, and blue.

The fact is that no matter how we describe them, these are the six that mingle and mix. Once you know them and understand them, you will be able to start figuring out what colors you want, must have, or have to keep away from in order to make perfect color out of your treasures.

The physics of color is one big complicated enchilada that is responsible for explaining the science of light along with the sense of sight. As light hits an object, all the colors in the rainbow hit at once, and only the ones that are not absorbed reflect back so our eyes can tell our brains what color we are seeing.

Although you are able to see thousands of variations of red, green, purple, orange, blue, and green through light, distance, and surfaces, there are still only those six colors that register in your brain.

The six colors deliver such an emotional punch that we become masochists at heart. "Hit me baby one more time" is what we want out of the feelings we get from color. We call these six by many different names with the hope that somehow we can make it clear about the "kind" of yellow or red we want. Why do we want to make it clear? We all have different emotional requirements that need to be individually met. There are only six but the thousands of variations confuse us into thinking we have to worry about all of them.

No other industry indulges these fantasies more than the paint industry. It's not done on purpose; they just want to make sure that if you can imagine it, you can have it. But when you are actually bombarded with too many color choices, it is hard to remember what the color really is and thus you begin to doubt how many there really are. After all, if there are 172 blues to look at, how can you even *imagine* the oasis? Your oasis is two blues at the most!

If the paint store turned into a clothing store, no one could shop. Imagine the fear behind making choices from the store that offers infinite shades of the same color.

My clients often call just days before the painters get there.

She was tired from sleepless nights knowing she had to make a decision about the wall colors. Her husband couldn't take it any more, not one more day. The indecision was killing every minute of their free time. It was a conversation that consumed them. "What do you think of..." would start in a curious tone and end with a level of frustration he was not willing to spend one more waking moment on. JUST PICK ONE! was the final ultimatum.

Well, how could she pick one out of thousands of choices that now seemed all wrong? She loved red but never on a wall. She could do green but that was too boring and besides, she had already done green in all the other previous homes. She had tried every taupe she could find and they were all dirty and pink. She had a couple of yellows but why should she do yellow? The more she looked for simple solutions that were supposed to pull it all together, the more she was crazy-quilting her home. Then her friends stepped in with every piece of color advice they had ever heard. *"Red would be too loud." "You should do the green and be done." "I personally love blue."* So it is not only about the color in your head, it is about the experience others will have with it.

When I got there, I took a deep breath and began to explain, starting with the basics. Red, yellow, orange, blue, green, and purple are the six colors of the rainbow that bounce all over the place. What we needed to do was call each of her things by a color. The floor was not really oak, it was orange; the couch was not really cream, it was yellow; and the counter tops were not really gray, they were blue. So what would go with orange, yellow, and blue?

Sometimes, it's simply a matter of elimination.

Well, she was obviously not a purple lover as nothing there was purple. That eliminated one color. So how about red, yellow, or green? Why? There was already too much orange overtaking the space with the oak floors. That eliminated orange. Yellow would be a color that all the other colors would have a good relationship with, and red or green would make great relationships. Blue could always be a small splash as an accent. Sometimes, it's simply a matter of elimination.

She never dreamed that the red (Devine Saffron) could be so stunning in the room with lots of cabinets and windows. She found the yellow (Devine Ray) going throughout the home was the "unifying neutral" popping out all the greens and reds. And as for the greens she loved (Devine Olive), they found a place in her home again. She never told her husband she paid me to consult until it was all done. He was thrilled that she had found not only ONE color that worked, but several. You often found him at parties talking about not just the ONE color his wife chose but the many colors that we selected that made the difference. They were perfect!

Once you think of playing around with only six colors, it makes it a lot easier to find the colors you want to go with the colors you have. You will then end up with the colors you love.

Look around and start to play the game of "what's that color?" Keep forcing yourself to call everything one of the six and pretty soon when you begin to imagine that your oasis needs that perfect blue, you will be able to find it!

Your Turn

Now that you know that there are only six colors, go around the entire main area of your home and start naming everything you see by one of the six colors in the rainbow. Take a long hard look. If you can't see which color it is at first, start calling it by which color it is not.

Make all things hostage to one of the six colors — your wood floors and cabinets, surfaces, fabrics, art, everything large or important. See if you can find a pattern of color you're attracted to, even in the things you never considered to have an actual color. Something to be aware of — a color may seem to be a combination of colors such as reddish orange, but adjacent to the other things in your home, the orange may be stronger next to the reds that are present. Therefore, in your home that color would be orange, not red.

"NEUTRAL COLORS ARE SAFE"

NEUTRALS ARE DANGEROUS

LET'S GET ONE THING straight, there are no taupes, grays, or beiges in the rainbow and you know what that means? They are not colors. Yet somehow we keep talking about them like they really are. Why? Because they make us sound decisive without having to make actual decisions. These are often used as the blanket answer when you want open options about color. In other words, they are safe. If you do taupe, hopefully you don't have to worry about it making a statement, clashing, matching, or dominating. We are all afraid of commitment.

There is a reason why we want to buy neutrals and it works. It keeps the options open. We all want to feel like we have options to change our minds, and not have to spend more or make room for mistakes. One evening when I was watching *Sleepless in Se-*

attle, I realized that the character Meg Ryan was going to marry was a neutral. Here she was playing it safe and yet, Walter the neutral would have eventually surprised her in a big way with his quiet, safe characteristics. What she thought was harmless would quietly clash with her enough to drive her insane. Luckily she escaped this fate. The whole movie is about magic.

These so-called safe colors can blow up in your face. They leave you in shock and you can't believe you didn't see the color coming. You keep playing the scenario over and over again. You looked at all the carpet samples, and the choice to you was very clear. You picked a neutral that would go with everything you have. Something along the sounds of Pebble Stone or Ivory Tower.

As a matter of fact, you picked a neutral because you wanted to ignore it altogether. Somewhere along the line, neutral colors became the "color filler" of color. We think of them as being more natural, like nature. They are thought of as color without color, just ambiance, that is until the carpet you bought is down and, KABOOM! Surprise, there goes ambiance and here comes green. At first you don't realize that it is green, you just know something is way off. It clashes, looks gray, or looks just plain wrong. The more you look at it with the couch and the oak floors, the more you see the faint lime green in it.

The worst part is that you can't keep your eyes off of it. Here is the very thing you wanted to be invisible and now it is clearer than ever. So the words "ignore the carpet" are always in the brain.

You want to hear the big surprise? KABOOM, all neutrals have color. They have within them the six colors of the rainbow wrestling with each other, mixing with one another so much so that they cancel each other out and make mud. But even mud has a color.

As the light hits, all the colors are shaking and baking together, much like salt and pepper in the same bag goes from black and white to gray. So here you think you have picked a color that has no color and all of a sudden something pops out of it like the green in the carpet that makes you clearly see you have just made a big expensive mistake. There goes non-commitment, spending less, and staying clear of mistakes.

Neutrals are considered safe because they are not supposed to engage with other colors. But because they have col-

Neutrals are considered safe because they are not supposed to engage with other colors. But because they have colors in them, they do engage. Color always engages with your eyes, with the object you are seeing, and with the colors around it.

ors in them, they do engage. Color always engages with your eyes, with the object you are seeing, and with the colors around it.

With all the colors you see day in and day out, the colors in the neutrals are often overpowered by the more dominant colors around them and therefore they seem colorless. In nature, you don't notice them as a color or get surprised by a color because they are in the perfect color combinations that let your eyes accept the color within them.

To find out if your neutral has the right color in it, you have to "interview" it for the job. When you interview a person for a job, you don't want to ask them questions that lead to a yes or no answer. You want to ask them situational questions.

The way to interview a neutral to find yellow, green, red, purple, blue, or orange in it is to put it in a particular situation. You don't ask if it is light or dark or warm. You ask it, "Next to a red chair, will you be turning blue? Purple? Orange? If I put you with greens, are you going to be yellow or green?" If it doesn't answer, then let's talk about what it won't do in the situation. "Will you promise not to go pink next to the blue? Can you stay green if I put you next to another stronger green?"

Go through the list; if the neutral is not orange, yellow, blue, or green, then it has to be purple or red. If it goes kind of grayish, it might begin to look purple. If it goes more pinkish, then the red is popping out. To make sure, put the neutral that you have now identified as red or purple in a situation where you hold it next to another color and watch to see if it changes. Does it stay red or become more purple? The thrill is to see the changing colors that emerge from underneath the neutral, depending on what's around. Clearly, it's helpful to have healthy samples of new materials you might be considering to compare with what you have.

KABOOM, neutrals can change, and this makes them volatile or flexible depending on if you think the glass is half empty or full. You decide as long as you are looking at them next to the glass.

KABOOM, neutrals can change, and this makes them volatile or flexible depending on if you think the glass is half empty or full. You decide as long as you are looking at them next to the glass.

Take that pink taupe that really is red and put it next to lots of other red shades and it may turn green. KABOOM, you just got hit again by surprise. But really, you have just begun to learn how to play fair with neutrals so they play by your rules, your things, and your world.

I was at a luncheon once where the hostess was truly gifted at home engineering. Great food, great wine, and great style defined her almost perfect world. It was *almost* because while she had many things she was happy about, the wall color had been a problem. She told me how she had worked on the wall color for weeks and that finally she had been able to find a light taupe that she was happy with and that went with everything.

But as the day wore on and the champagne flowed, she began to spill her guts about the absolute nightmare it really was to actually get that flipping color that she had worked so hard at matching at the paint store because the guy behind the counter couldn't get it right and that it was not really the color she wanted but she had settled for it even though it ended up slightly colder than she expected and so on. This was like basically saying she married him because she couldn't find anyone else. So then she asked, "What do you think of the color?" It was a set-up.

I was being set up because on one hand, there was nothing wrong with the way the home looked and by all accounts it was head and shoulders above most homes. But on the other hand, we both knew there was a pink elephant in the room and she wanted to see if I saw it. (Note to self: if I ever hear someone say do you think my hair is too short, it is because they think their

hair is too short and they want you to say it is not! It's a set-up.)

I had to answer the color question knowing that she wanted to hear that her world was perfect. I said the reason why the color felt a little cold to her was probably the fact that she had purple on the walls and her furniture and fabrics were more in the red-orange-yellows so maybe the purple was causing the problem.

Of course I got the response I was expecting. She thought I was on crack. I obviously was not as good a color consultant as she had heard. Her taupe was not purple, she said, it was slightly gray but she wouldn't call it purple; she called it taupe, a cool taupe.

I then asked her to look at the corner where the floor color and the kitchen cabinets met (the situation). Then (the interview), what color is the wall turning next to the floor that is orange and the cabinets that are yellow? I played the "let's pretend" game that everything has color and you have to name everything one of the six colors of the rainbow. She stopped and was thinking...

I said, "Let me put it this way. The walls do not look green, yellow, or orange, right? And they are not red because it is not pink as much as it is purple. There under the seemingly gray cast this purple hue surfaced, now so evident, she couldn't take her eyes off it. She saw it for the first time and once it caught her eye, it was everywhere. Her pink elephant was actually purple.

As she looked at her pillows and accessories, the walls kept getting more and more purple. Her painters came out that same week to replace purple with neutral green (Devine Pecan) that read like a rich khaki. The reds, golds, and oranges in her home now had a cooler "neutral" on the walls to balance all the warm colors. But it was a green and not a purple that would do the job.

After all, if one of the six colors in the rainbow is going to keep popping up no matter what, you might as well have control of what pops out. Being able to find the color within the neutrals is the answer.

I ended up developing neutrals that you could work with as color and not as insurance; they support other colors as a silent partner but are never less than a color. Remember only color can make perfect relationships between your things.

The next time you are looking at a neutral, anticipate the surprise. Look for the color underneath the neutral. If you can't see the color — if it's not yellow, orange, blue, green, or purple — trust me, it's red and has the potential to explode as one big pink flesh bomb. KABOOM!

"I WANTED CARAMEL, NOT CAMEL"

COLORS ARE NOT THINGS, THINGS HAVE COLOR

IT WAS A BIG deal when Isaac Newton discovered that color did not belong to objects but to light. Having said that, it does not mean we sleep better because of it. A conversation along these lines might go like this: Did you mean plum, pinot, eggplant, blackberry, amethyst, or lavender? Why can't it be just purple? In order to blend or contrast your colors successfully, you need to see past the romance of the words.

Colors are on everything we see. The fact that each color of the rainbow can be described in terms of so many fruits, vegetables, and nuts makes a complicated trail mix between how we see and how we understand.

Yet with someone who is green with envy, we seem to have no problem knowing what the green looks like. We don't define the kind of jealousy by different shades of it, like being jealous enough to be sage but not mint. Try telling someone you are doing jealousy green on the wall, and no one knows what that means, or they know it can only mean one green. Confusion takes over. Green as jealousy is one thing; as wall color it's another.

This is why, when you want to paint it red, what comes to mind is the kind of red we are scared of because what pops into your head are crazy possibilities like fire-engine, clown, or whore red. Same goes for orange (fruit), purple (Barney) or yellow (lemon). Since our brains immediately reach inside our kid color file when we say the name, we rely on things around us to verbally explain what type of color we actually want.

The problem is that once you call a green-yellow pillow, for example, by the name of lima bean, you run the risk of forgetting it is yellow as well as green. So when you buy this color and you bring it home as a green and put it with all the other greens, it looks like it threw up all over itself.

There is a happy medium between talking about the kind of color we want while calling out the color it actually is. After all, caramel is an orange-red with hints of green, whereas camel is an orange-yellow with a hint of red. Yet you could imagine them both being the same and tripping us up the next time we were buying the actual yellow color. I could have ended up in a sherbet disaster had my man Isaac Newton not clarified all the colors of the rainbow.

I'm in a store and I am looking at the greatest couch for sale I have ever seen. It's a suede-looking sofa in two tones of orange. I compliment the designer on the orange sofa. The sales person quickly corrects me by saying that it is not orange, but melon with coral trim. If I didn't know any better, I would be buying a piece of fruit with an ocean rock to sit on.

But it was really important not be seduced by the engaging words of marketing because I needed to remind myself that this was an orange-red color. I had a different orange to deal with at home. My walls were wall-to-wall clear hemlock built by an architect in the early sixties with a 14-foot wall with cathedral windows and cedar tongue-and-groove ceilings. Orange, right?

I let her know that I had wood walls in my home. She thought that the beautiful couch would be great in my warm, cozy environment. While a coral, melon couch in a hemlock living room sounds very warm and pretty, the orange hemlock wood had a lot of green. If I was not careful, the oranges in the sofa would have looked pink and fleshy with the wood at home.

I didn't buy the couch since the oranges would have clashed. Had I not known the actual color I was looking at, this would have been an expensive mistake.

All I'm saying is that it is very important to know what you are seeing, and kids are really good at calling it like it is. Children are the first ones to look at something and call it simply by its color. They still are being weaned by the crayon box that teaches them to put the color on the object.

I remember a particular family that was genuine and absolutely lovely. A member of this family taught me to call it what you want as long as you know what you are getting. They had invested their lives in their kids and you could see they were amazing parents. They had sports equipment everywhere, jumping dogs, and old cats. They had friends, vacations and scrapbooking. They had Boy Scouts, Brownies, and poker.

We set up a time to meet in the early evening. The entire family was very interested and curious about what I was going to do for them. During the conversation, I was trying to describe a color that was a cool, soft, light putty with green warm gray hues that seemed well-worn.

In the kid world, there is

no such thing. They are still in a pop-sicle world. They know the rainbow better than anyone else. Their nine-year-old kid was trying to understand what the heck I was trying to describe as a color. It was no popsicle he had ever heard of. So he looked at the well-trav-eled floor and asked if the color I was talking about was close to the color that was in the cat barf stain on the carpet? I quickly answered yes, but that I wanted it more purple and slightly darker. Ah-hhhh, they all said.

We went about our color business without skipping a beat. They knew it as soon as they saw the cat barf stain the color I was talking about, even though I was still defining how I saw color.

We won't stop looking for things that try to define the colors we are imagining, but we have to make our eyes see past what it is, like whether the yellow we are looking at is yellow, or yellow-orange, or orange with red, or orange with a hint of green turning it mustard.

We won't stop looking for things that try to define the colors we are imagining, but we have to make our eyes see past what it is, like whether the yellow we are looking at is yellow, or yellow-orange, or orange with red, or orange with a hint of green turning it mustard.

"I HAVE TO HAVE THAT COLOR"

NOT IF YOU DON'T KNOW WHERE TO PUT IT

BELIEVE IT OR NOT I have gone into homes before to take away color. The clients just had to have a certain color so they used so much of it they ran out of places to put it. It seems that because we react so strongly to particular colors we love, we think we should have them anywhere and everywhere. Let me tell you about a client of mine who didn't refuse herself anything when it came to either shoes or the color yellow.

She had tried 12 shades of yellow by the time I had gotten there. She wanted a yellow kitchen. Somewhere in her imagination she knew what the room was going to feel like, look like, and say about her once she got it. She thought only yellow could bring in the warmth she was looking for. She couldn't wait to put up all her red accents, like dishes and platters, to go with it.

All the yellows she had tried would turn a little green, a little pink, too orange, dirty, sallow, pale, lemon, or anemic next to the other things in her home. She couldn't understand why she couldn't find *the* yellow and every time she thought she had it, it was wrong. She thought as a color expert I would be able to help her find the right yellow that would let her have exactly what she had in mind. This is where having the right place for the right color is so important. There was so much yellow in the room already because of all the maple cabinets and hardwood floors that adding more yellow was way too much.

It was a clear case of too much of a good thing can make you sick, like too many Lemon Drops. Only other colors would make the existing yellow work. Why shouldn't she have yellow? There was no place to really put it. If she stacked it on top of all the yellows already there, your eyes would have been too full.

She was so surprised how she had struggled to find the exact yellow, only to find out it was there all along, in plain sight, and she had missed it. When you've decided on a color, you have to ask yourself if it is already in the room, how much of it is there, and finally, where else could it be placed?

It all boiled down to one thing. No yellow in the world would have worked; she would

It was a clear case of too much of a good thing can make you sick, like too many Lemon Drops.

have to go with one of the other colors in the rainbow list. I had to take her color away from her. This was no place for more is more; more was too much.

More is often too much. Whenever I would go shopping and find things on sale, I would always think I had to have "it" but where would I put it? "A place for each thing," a friend of mine used to say, "that is how you decide if you buy it or not. If you can't find a place for things, they begin to stack up and pretty soon, you don't own them, they own you."

This is true of memories so why not keep the good ones in your good file and a couple of bad ones for a rainy day and be done. But don't live your life constantly remembering the past.

This is also true of magazines. I have a big secret to tell you; they are making more where those came from. Every month. The ideas are reworked and reworked over and over again. And if you miss the idea of the century, don't worry. The idea will be copied to death by everyone so you will see it done again and again.

Of course we need to find the colors we love because we are looking for them to be good partners to our other things. The tie has to go with the shirt and the suit; the dress has to have a cardigan; the table has to have a lamp and so forth. No matter what, you are constantly looking for the next color to fit with or next to whatever you have.

The problem is our one-track mind. It's like a horse with blinders; you only see the color in front of you and not what's around. Had that woman looked at the yellows that were already in place, she would have looked for what they needed, not what she thought she wanted.

What you need can come as a real big surprise. I was once doing a home where the owners loved color. So much so they had lots of it and it was actually a very exciting and interesting space. It was perfect color.

However, they had painted themselves into a corner. They loved color and already had the color they loved in the things they had. They loved yellow and they already had plenty of it, so what they needed was not more yellow, but actually a color that would pop that yellow so they could see it bright and clear. They needed a neutral with lots of richness and heaviness.

I wanted to put a rich chocolate called Devine Cocoa on all the walls. Not only did I want to do this rich dark color there, but I wanted it to come out to the hallway so it could actually start un-

A picture of many colors proclaims images of many thoughts.

~ Donna A. Favors

Color needs a place and it needs to be in good company. It is not monogamous.

der the white staircase molding in the entryway, making the two rooms connect and double in size visually.

The clients were freaking out. "The color is too dark, maybe not even a color! What about red, blue, yellow, or purple?"

No, there was already too much of it in all that they owned and the walls had to act as a showcase for all of their colorful things. It was all about adding a neutralizing color so it would complement all the relationships already in existence. You have to have evil (contrast) to have good (harmony). This is how you win the battle, this is how good wins!

Color needs a place and it needs to be in good company. It is not monogamous.

It was not about taking color away, it was about asking what colors were already there, how much was there, and where should they be placed.

Believe me, you want the right thoughts with that many colors. In that home, the addition of more bold and dazzling colors would have ruined the perfect balance they had created. It would have gone from exciting and interesting to loud and annoying.

Colors can be hard to determine, but

Colors can be hard to determine, but never hard to find as long as you are looking for them as the right partners in the right amounts. Think about balance and proportion.

never hard to find as long as you are looking for them as the right partners in the right amounts. Think about balance and proportion.

The world we walk into everyday through our front door needs to give us not only perfect beauty through color but a sense of knowing we are living with what we love. Take a moment and look at your things in your home and find the colors that are there, see how much of it there is, and look for colors that should be added to make all of them perfect.

Your Turn

Make a rainbow pie. Take a look at each room you have and make a drawing of a pie. Give each color in the room its proportional slice of the pie. You can group the neutrals in one slice, as well as all variations of each color. (Example: different yellows in one slice including maple wood, a yellow couch, and a sunflower print.) You now have a pie that could look like this — 65% yellow, 5% green, and 5% purple. So what colors should you bring in to build a lovely relationship with these pie slices?

Now ask yourself what color needs to be bigger, smaller, or added to make the combination all taste delicious. If you wanted to have a different color in the room and there is no more room in the pie, leave it alone and move on to the next pie or take out a slice and replace.

"I LOVE THAT COLOR"

YOU LOVE THOSE COLORS

RECEIVING LOVE MAKES YOU happy, but the act of giving love is much more satisfying and affirming. Think about it. They say you can survive a marriage where both people are in love or both people are out of love, but when one person receives but does not give, that is when it's over. We all want to fall in love, and of course be in love — forever. That is what would happen in a perfect world.

That happy feeling you get from a favorite color comes from your brain replaying over and over again the moment you first fell in love with that color. It could have been a shirt, a place, or a crayon. My friend always tells the story how she fell in love with red the first time she saw her red fingernails against her porcelain white skin. Her hands looked beautiful. To this day, all her dishes are red, her pillows are red, and she has to stop herself from buying more! When you have a favorite color, it is like an addiction. You impulsively buy it, wear it, and have to tell others about it. You know why you have to have it? Because it is all about you.

I remember falling in love with green emeralds I once saw in a jewelry store. Among all the various colors I loved the green the most because of how it looked with yellow gold. I desperately wanted that green so it became my color. I asked for green popsicles, culottes, ribbons, and costumes. I loved being a green elf in the Christmas pageant. When it came time to go to the *quinceañeras* (a formal fifteenth-birthday extravaganza) for all my friends in Puerto Rico, my grandmother would go to the store and buy these beautiful chiffon fabrics to make me stunning formal dresses in different shades of green, from emerald, to kelly to aqua to chartreuse. (Yes, that is how I ended up making liquid chiffon in gallons so the colors would look rich and luxurious.) When you love a color it makes you happy.

> I cannot pretend to feel impartial about colors. I rejoice with the brilliant ones, and am genuinely sorry for the poor browns.
>
> ~ Winston Churchill

My love for green became the love affair with lime green I can't live without. Whether conscious of this love or not, I've had that color around in some form or another all my adult life. I have had to explain it to everyone. I'm sure some of you have experienced the same feeling for a color that you love when others don't feel the same way about it. In Puerto Rico, nature had every variation of bright green and of course sparkling lime greens. In the water, on rocks, moss, on leaves, birds, even in the skyline reflection of the sunset, lime green would sneak up and absolutely shine with brilliance. The sun turned greens into yellows with its powerful light. The ocean blue made the yellows even brighter so the spectacle of it all was delicious to my eyes.

When I moved to the Northwest, I came to a place with lots of greens as well. Our climate makes our nature as luscious and evergreen as the tropics, with one minor difference — the sun. The greens in Puerto Rico had this supporting cast of other colors that made them stunning to everyone who saw them.

In the Northwest, the greens were mossy, shadowy, grayer, bluer, silver, and deeper. They were beautiful, with rich bark, gray winter skies, a rugged coastline and lots and lots of evergreens. So needless to say, trying to explain lime green as a great color with no crisp blues, corals, whites, oranges, turquoises, sea shells, palms, sand, reefs, bananas, and birds of paradise around was a little hard. It seemed out of place. When you love a color, the feeling it gives you is personal because your experience of it among others is just as important.

Funny, because while most kids have a ferocious passion to hang on to the color they love, adults sometimes have a hard time fitting it in when they get older.

Love affairs can last a lifetime. But as trends come and go, our love for a color gets displaced by the new, improved colors of the time. The color we love begins to disappear among others that come into fashion. It is hard to keep the flame of love alive, especially when others keep blowing it out!

Mauve was so hot in the eighties. It was feminine, yet strong enough for men to live with. It had the perfect partners in blues and "tans." Another trend story of the time was peach, partnering with its greens and "creams." It all seemed perfect. You had the "cool" palette for the "cool" people and the "warm" palette for "warm" people. As the suburbs were growing and sprawling across the nation, these colors were growing with them in a way that color had never spread before.

It all seemed so easy until new trendy color combos came into the scene replacing mauve, tan, blues, and creams with jewel-tones of cobalt blues, hunter

> Funny, because while most kids have a ferocious passion to hang on to the color they love, adults sometimes have a hard time fitting it in when they get older.

greens, and cranberry reds with crisp white. There is that moment when you quietly stop talking about the color you love. Don't believe me? OK, where have all the mauve people gone?

In suburbia everyone wants to fit in and be affirmed. The neighbors are close, the homes are close to being the same, and everyone hopes to have similar interests. Why else would you form neighborhood organizations, book clubs, do progressive dinners, and play Bunco? It is hard to go against the tide.

Builders caught on and in an attempt to sell homes in these suburban clusters, the designers accented with the trend colors of the time. Unfortunately, this resulted in time capsules that dated everything. Later new homes were offered with a sea of noncommittal neutrals to combine with the next merry-go-round colors. The problem I saw was that following so many trends, so many color mistakes, and so much confusion as to what was the right thing to do with color, nobody remembered or wanted to admit to what they loved.

One client had me build a color palette in one of these brand new homes in a very expensive suburb. It was very upscale, and even if some plans were repeated throughout the neighborhood, the buyers were given upgrades with choices to make them more individual.

I had the client absolutely in love with the idea of painting the high den ceiling a beautiful blue. It was a cove ceiling that had crown molding accented by lights. It was the perfect color to balance the walls and create an amazing canopy above a perfect "think tank."

The call came in a week later. She loved the color and as a matter of fact, it was a great way to introduce a color that she had loved before. It went great with her artwork and it was present in bits and pieces in the things she and her husband had collected throughout the years. But there was one thing that made her rethink it. The builder had really questioned her decision. As a matter of fact he thought it was kind of crazy. My client lost her confidence right away. I asked her if she had ever been to her builder's home. She said no. I asked her if she knew what he would wear out to dinner. No again.

It's funny because even though she thought it was a great idea, believed in it, and had loved the color all her life, the lack of affirmation and doubts from a builder whom she didn't even know affected her confidence. Of course, she went against her own feelings and my advice and didn't have the ceiling painted blue. She later told me she re-

The story of Little Blue Riding Hood is true. Only the color has been changed to prevent an investigation.

~ Stan Freberg

gretted it. You can come up with a thousand reasons, but when the reason for a decision is because you love it, that is always the only one that counts.

She understood how bland and uninteresting the room looked and how a striking color in that location would have given it great interest, amazing detail, and a fun element of surprise.

In her mind, she would always see that ceiling in blue. When you go into a home and find odd pieces of color in art or fabrics that are tucked away in guest bedrooms, theme rooms, or private masters — you can feel these colors mattered to someone at some point. Often these colors are found in meaningful collections — colors that people have been in love with, but no longer fit it in with the others they now have.

When you go into a home and find odd pieces of color in art or fabrics that are tucked away in guest bedrooms, theme rooms, or private masters — you can feel these colors mattered to someone at some point.

This is when I remind them that these personal treasures also contain the six colors in the rainbow and we can actually make them seem part of their new world, not some leftover color remnant from their past. Remember that color is perfect as long as it has the right partners and the right place, even if it is blue on the ceiling.

So what is the right place for a color? This has to do with the purpose of creating interest, dimension, or simply just stunning beauty. My client's blue ceiling was intended to bring excitement and the beauty of a loved color to an already stunning feature in the room, the cove ceiling.

The jewel-tone people are still around hiding under the blanket of Tuscany reds and yellows.

The jewel-tone people are still around hiding under the blanket of Tuscany reds and yellows.

Just the other day, I found one of the closeted jewel-toners during the training I give my color consultants. One of these training classes turned up a person who had gone undercover with her favorite colors and had transitioned to what was now current. At first it was not as obvious. She had a navy blue leather set in the family room, and some cranberry splashes here and there but her home had lots of the newer warm reds, golds, and creams.

She was showing me the fabrics for the window treatments that she was having delivered. I was ready to take her into wall colors when I happened to mention to her that because she loved jewel tones, I would make sure her wall colors made them work with all the other colors she was buying. The consultants in training were a bit confused. "Aren't we supposed to match what is here?"

one said. "The home is not really full of jewel tones!"

It was not full of jewel tones, but you could see that even though she had moved on to trend colors, there were clues everywhere that were not to be ignored. Almost like color DNA. I pointed out that the navy couches really picked up on the blues, teals, and pink reds in the pictures on the walls. You could see deep purples peeking out of prints in pillows. The cranberry master bedding was a dead giveaway. The client opened right up about how much she had always loved those colors, so much so that she couldn't part with those smaller items with colors in them she loved. Her challenge was to try to hang onto them as they seemed to be washed over with new waves of incoming color. The colors I chose for her allowed her to live in both worlds without losing what she loved.

The six colors to the rainbow can be combined to make the colors you love, want, and have to live with fit as a perfect picture of who you are. Like I said, it is all about you. There is a color you love and loving it makes you feel like no other.

I want at least a small bite of the color you love for you in every room so you feel full and satisfied.

Let's say you love blue and you always have, especially next to white. Purple becomes trendy and you start bringing it into the home. You might find the blue you love looks depressing with it. So you start taking the blue out and replace it with greens and reds to go with the purple. It all looks great but you are not sure why you don't feel as happy in the room as when you walk into the bathroom with all the old blue and white colors.

Looking at the blue with just the purple as a partner confused everything! If you wanted a purple couch instead of a blue and white one, the blue and white could have stayed around in the room as art or accessories. Having a color you love that continues to love you back in every room is what gives you that great happy gift.

Throughout decades, my favorite greens came and went in many versions. Once paired up with harvest gold as avocado, in the nineties as jade paired up with salmon, I now have it as lime with blues and chocolates. In every room I have a little of it peeking out of patterns, rugs, and glass I have collected as my color treasures. This is what sets my home apart.

> You can't be at the pole and the equator at the same time. You must choose your own line, as I hope to do, and it will probably be color.
>
> ~ Vincent Van Gogh

You can still have your cake and eat it too by making sure that the color you love is around, even if it is in small doses. Look around and you will see variations, translations, adaptations, and transformations of the same colors. Make sure that the one that you are really crazy about is one of them.

I want at least a small bite of the color you love for you in every room so you feel full and satisfied.

Your Turn

Take a look at the color you love right now in this moment, and see what else it is paired up with in your home. Look at fabrics, clothing, art, or even books. Is there a color relationship you like better than another? Is there a color relationship that makes the color you love stand out to you more? Is there a color relationship that reminds you of past things you hold dear? Is there a time when one color is paired with another and you don't like it?

"I HATE THAT COLOR"

YES, YOU DO

IF SOMEONE AT A party says they hate yellow and someone else pipes in to say they hate it too, they are both relieved and happy that not only does another person agree, but that they are right. So, conversely, if you like it, it must mean you are stupid! Yes, the power in numbers is the junior high mentality we all revert to when it comes to wanting someone to agree with us that something is good or bad. It has to do with insecurities we all carry around from a painful childhood. Color becomes one of those things that stand out very clearly in our minds when we think of a lot of these rejections.

Many of us can clearly remember a time in junior high when we stood out and were made fun of. Like when my oldest daughter became a seventh grader and wanted to stay a kid a little longer. It was her birthday and she and her friends were all going to the Avril Levigne concert. She wanted to wear these crazy-colored striped socks with shorts and a Superman t-shirt. It was colorful all right and fun till she met up with all her friends.

They were all in white tank-tops, jeans, and straight hair. My daughter had curled hers for the occasion. She stood out like colored Christmas lights out of season. You could feel the rejection in the air. I took a picture of them that day and drove home crying. But please wipe your tears. She was homecoming princess in the ninth grade and has gone on to be an amazing, beautiful, and independent thinker.

All we want to do in life is to be understood, and there are colors that we hate because they represent an event that changed our minds about it. Just like a color you love stands out in your mind, so does one you hate.

When you ask someone about a color they hate, the stories are endless. In some instances there was even emotional damage. These stories are so personal — they beg for someone else to tell them, it is OK to hate that color. After all, nobody wants to hate anything, let alone something as frivolous as this.

The pink dress her mother made her wear to parties is now the reason she wears black all the time;

it drives her mother nuts. The green peas on the plate you had to finish are now the color you can't even buy on a plant. The orange that you relate to the "clown" incident is something you are still not ready to talk about.

My grandmother always hated purple. When I was a child she would always hate to see me cold and would make it clear in a very disapproving tone that my lips were purple, not cold, PURPLE.

I thought the purple thing had to do with me getting cold but years later, she had a cataract removed and she called me in a panic. She was so upset at this vase that she had always seen as a cool, dark charcoal. Now that her vision had been unveiled, she was shocked and in horror that she had been living with purple.

She was always afraid of the sea and living in Puerto Rico her feelings were known every day as I headed to the beaches of San Juan. You see, she had seen a tourist drown as a child and when they pulled the body out of the water in front of her, it was purple. From then on, she just didn't like to look at purple.

Nature intends to deliver us from our own color prejudices. We can visualize how all colors can look beautiful together, particularly in nature. But because we do not live with nature inside, no matter how many stunning colors we enjoy outside, the ones we invite in are the ones that count. This means no hated colors are acceptable, even if they seem like a reasonable solution.

One young couple that had me over to their home was a great example of this. They had just gotten their new home in the suburbs. They were ready to transition from their IKEA furniture. They wanted this home to be a place where roots could be established and their adult life could begin. I walked by their living room and went into their family room/kitchen, which they had furnished and painted first to feel like home.

We now needed to choose colors for the rest of the house. I asked if we could start in the "orphan room," the one that looked like it didn't have a father or a mother. We all laughed because they knew which one I was talking about. The living room. This was where their leftover furniture had ended up and it looked like it had been abandoned. It had white walls, and a neutral called Devine Shell was going to do just the trick to warm things up. This color was going to replace all the remaining white so

we could then add some beautiful yellows, greens, and reds to make it all
work. The husband loved Devine Shell
because it was rich, creamy, and sophisticated.

She didn't. The color was beautiful and it looked great but she hated it. If either one of them hated a color, no matter how much the other one loved it, we couldn't build a palette with that color. Another choice was to move on to real color, and the white could be replaced with yellow. Devine Butter was the perfect choice. This would mean that having this much yellow would then allow for the reds and greens and blues to be very bright. YES! YES! YES! This was it. Ahhhh, to hear it sing!

She was in love with it and so he liked yellow. They already had tons of yellows, and things that went with yellow. As a matter of fact, Devine Shell did go with yellow but it was not yellow enough for her. I talked to her about how she felt about neutral colors in general and she said she hated beige. She didn't want to end up with a beige house and having Devine Shell in over half of her home would give her a terrible feeling.

I asked her if she remembered hating beige for the first time and she proceeded to tell me that when her parents got divorced, she lived in so many apartments with her mom that she ended up hating neutrals. They gave her a transient feeling. This woman was looking for roots; she really didn't want to be orphaned anymore.

After all, she had been renting all her single life and part of her married life, so she had been waiting to be able to buy a home to make it a reflection of her personality and tastes, along with her husband's. Beige was not personal. This is where she planned to start her family.

It is OK to hate a color because it always boils down to a personal experience. It is that experience that needs to be shared to understand how color is such an integral part of our love-hate relationship with our surroundings.

It is OK to hate a color because it always boils down to a personal experience. It is that experience that needs to be shared to understand how color is such an integral part of our love-hate relationship with our surroundings.

The six colors of the rainbow are all around us, and the magic of light lets us see them in outrageous and perfect combinations. I know my grandmother would never take the purple out of a sunset or a vineyard even if she hated purple.

When we all see colors in relationship to one another with meaning and purpose, somehow our eyes take over and let us accept them and like them even though they would personally drive us crazy if we lived with them. After all, my grandmother changed many things around the house but she didn't get rid of the green and purple plastic grapes for a long time.

Your Turn

It is hard to accept the fact there is a color you hate, so pick one. Now, take a look at the personal reasons the color is conflicting to you. For example, I know a woman who associated pink with cheap wallpaper and therefore it took her a long time to accept that the color could be luxurious, or so she tells herself when she sees it come and go in fashion after confessing her story. Believe me, there is a story to be told somewhere in the recesses of your mind. Then think of three ways that colors are used in other relationships where, in combination, they make one another look beautiful. Think of a view in nature, a painting, a sculpture, or a rug. Look for those relationships to understand that color better and to become less judgmental.

"I don't have a favorite color"

You do have a favorite color

FAVORING A COLOR IS psychologically important to us because it allows us to have preference and that's all part of affirming our existence and individuality.

There is favoritism with color. It is how we start making sense of the world. Young ones favor a color without a care in the world about what others like. Color gives children opinions about what is theirs in the world and the one thing they can take immediate ownership of is color!

In checkers, kids know if they want red or black; in board games, colors are fought over before anyone gets to play. You could always see the unhappiness in a kid with the leftover color in Parcheesi nobody wanted.

> The purest and most thoughtful minds are those which love color the most.
>
> ~ John Ruskin

As a matter of fact, kids believe color is more important than things because they color outside the lines and a tree can be red and they can have orange grass. Such confidence lies in the crayon box that is always there waiting for them to be masters over every color, placing it wherever their little hearts desire.

By the time they are an adult, they want to have the same sense of wonder and freedom. But this time, the crayon box is no longer there. Colors come and go at someone else's whim and we find ourselves not getting too attached to any color because now color comes in a limited edition.

You love green but the crayon box this year has no greens in it. Instead the shirts now come in pimento, cayenne, pepper, pomegranate, raspberry, and next year it could be cherry, cardinal, maroon, coral, or crimson. But once you get used to the reds, they could be gone and replaced by another color, so you'd better not get too attached to anything.

As children we always knew the crayon box would be there again in the morning with all the colors. As adults, however, the box feels like it is gone and now you get what you get. I tell my clients that they are going to have to build their own crayon box with what is around. This is why I remind them of their favorite color, so they can begin to paint outside the lines and color their trees with it. The fun part of finding your favorite color is going through all the crayons in the box till the one you love is in your hands ready to paint the town carnation pink, cornflower, or midnight blue.

Finding your favorite color is the cheapest thrill you can have so take advantage of its guiltless pleasure.

It is never too late to start playing with the crayon box. I had a job in a retirement community with a couple who had been married for about a hundred years or so. Their daughter had recommended my services to them as an encouragement to take care of themselves. At the end of the color consultation they were thrilled with the colors that I picked.

They thought they had a hodge-podge of colors that did not really go together, but the things they had, they loved. Having given so much of themselves over to raising a family, this was the first time they had really contemplated the idea of a favorite color. The colors we ended up with went with everything from their past as well as their present.

They had not really paid attention to the fact that the things they loved did tell a color story and they had already built their own crayon box. It was all about them. Once the picture became clear,

> Finding your favorite color is the cheapest thrill you can have so take advantage of its guiltless pleasure.

it was as if they had done it purposefully. The husband was amazed at my certainty. He couldn't get over the fact that I was coming up with colors they had all over their home and how common they were in everything they had collected.

The wall colors would well serve as a support to what was already part of their home. They had already subconsciously chosen their favorite colors and I wanted to make them richer, fresher, and more beautiful. It was their favorite colors and their personal collections that mattered the most.

They were seeing their favorite colors as something that gave worth to what they owned. Later that year, after they had the colors painted, I heard from a neighbor that their daughter had seen such out-of-character excitement in her father that she thought the thrill was a lot less expensive and lasted longer than Viagra.

Don't be afraid of colors coming and going because your favorite is there among all the things you have already collected. You are going to have to play with color the old-fashioned way, like when you go through the crayon box and choose your favorite color among all others. I have such a strong belief about the power

They were seeing their favorite colors as something that gave worth to what they owned.

that color has over our lives that I built Devine Color as an adult crayon box for walls. It was important to have colors that tied everything together.

While some worry they do not even know what their favorite color is, others worry about having too many of them.

No one wants to wake up to a crayon box full of one color. Having your favorite color will not limit you, or make you stop loving all the others. Often when I show up at a home, I find some people who really want to bring in a color just because they don't want to do the same ones over and over again. It is almost as if they find themselves thinking that if they choose the same colors they are not adventurous.

I was in a couple's home who had done a great job at putting together great color. They already had Devine

Sand and Devine Terracotta throughout the house and by the names, I hope you can imagine the colors (or see them at www.devinecolor.com). They had purchased my services at a school auction to finish what they had started. These colors were paired up with lots of mossy greens, red dominant rugs, bird's eye maple, and light cherry furniture. If the house was a rainbow pie, I would say that the slices of orange, red, and yellow were pretty large pieces. They wanted a solution for their kitchen cabinets that coordinated with everything they had, especially the subway cream tiled walls and slate blue/green flooring in the kitchen original to the home.

I said the cabinets are going to be red. Wait a minute, the husband said, how could they be red? I always have a way to walk you through the decision. Let's deduct. They weren't going to be blue, purple, or green because the kitchen cabinets represented so large a proportion of space in the room that those colors would draw too much contrast and attention. We all agreed. So that left us with yellows, reds, and oranges. The yellow in the tile had a lot of icy green reflections so yellow cabinets would not POP the creamy look of it. Orange was not the right color to make it work, so there was only red left.

But we haven't really explored this, she said, why wouldn't we try a peachy color? Because I don't think either of us would wear that peachy color as a shirt if the pants were the color of those subway creamy yellow-green tiles. OK, what about an orange tone like the color of cherry wood, but in paint? It would compete with the beautiful bird's eye maple wood, I said.

So what kind of red are you talking about? The beautiful Devine Cayenne. The husband sighed, but why red, don't you think we have too much of it already? No, you already have the right amount in other rooms, and in this room, the right amount is also needed. That is why it is the best choice.

But why not another more surprising color? There is a difference between a surprise and shock. So-called surprising colors would look out of place. Since you have built this amazing crayon box that has red as the favorite color and other colors that support it, red in the kitchen becomes supportive to the subway tile and allows the original cool blue floor to be featured. There is already a color in the tile that is the "surprising color" for the room. His wife then says, so what you are saying is that choosing a color for a "surprise" would be like putting a baseball bat in your golf bag for playing golf. She was right! They would swing a great game of color with the right one.

The purest and most thoughtful minds are those which love color the most.

~ John Ruskin

Your Turn

The color you favor is the one that is the most personal. You will have variations of this color throughout your life, in different things with different names. It may not be the one most prominent in your life today, but it is the one that has an emotional connection to your past. Lucky are those whose favorite color is synonymous with love and who are able to live with it. See if you can remember your love affairs with different colors in your past and count the number of possessions that you still have as a result.

"IT'S JUST COLOR"

SOMETIMES IT'S ABOUT A LOT MORE

CONTEMPT PRIOR TO EXAMINATION is a color crime. Many color conversations are not just about color; they're about a lot more and somehow most people never talk about the "a lot more" part. This important part often gets left out.

How many times have you heard those sweet friends of yours say, "I don't get how you can like that color?" Well, what does that mean? They are not trying to make you feel bad, or make it seem as if you are committing some kind of crime against them or worse, yourself. They just don't seem to understand why that color would make you feel a certain way and not them.

They have eyes too, so *what do you see that they can't*? Often it is not what you see as much as what you feel.

A snooty girl with a lime green dress and white go-go boots stuck out her tongue at a good friend's husband in the sixth grade, crushing his crush and making him hate lime green, otherwise known as rejection green in his book.

For me, of course, lime green is love at first sight, otherwise known as the sunny green in my book. So why would I take his opinion of lime green and make it my own based on what we both see? I wouldn't.

Let me put it this way, my best friend's husband loves my house with lime green bits and pieces, loves to spend time in my house, and loves to sit on my lime green Adirondack chairs. Not once has he ever mentioned that this was his least favorite color because of that hip, pretty, trendsetting, go-go booted sixth grader until I was writing this book and asked.

In my home, lime green makes sense. I'm sure he has walked into homes where it is an out-of-place accessory representing a fashion trend, a color that comes and goes. He considers the color trendy but in my home he saw it as a cultural flavor to enjoy; in other places it reminded him of that trend-setting little blotch on his memory.

Color ownership comes from our upbringing, our heritage, and our experiences. Cultures can create a bias towards color through art, words, and ritual. Red in China means

Often it is not what you see as much as what you feel.

prosperity and protection, and white is associated with death. As a consequence, a Chinese bride wears red on her wedding day. In Western culture, red is associated with danger and white is purity and innocence. Hence, the tradition of brides wearing white!

> Mere color, unspoiled by meaning and unallied with definite form, can speak to the soul in a thousand different ways.
>
> ~ Oscar Wilde

Sometimes its meaning lies in what we think a color can do for us, like gangs who wear red to make them appear to be a family or black pants that make our butts look smaller.

I went with a group of women from my neighborhood to an art show with booths lined up featuring amazing paintings, pottery, and photography. I was attracted to several things that one of the women found impossible to like. "How can you like that? It looks crazy with all those colors."

I paused long enough to take a deep breath and seek higher ground so I wouldn't dropkick her. I said, "Look, have you ever seen the sky with baby blue, charcoal gray, orange and purple that then turns blazing red?"

She looked at this abstract painting that looked out of control to her and she said, well, now that you put it that way... But still, she said, she could never have it in her home. No one was asking her to. Everything she looked at was judged by how she felt. The problem is that she never asked why I felt the way that I did about those colors. Contempt prior to examination.

If she had, I would have told her that when I first moved to the Northwest, my favorite experience with nature was the sunsets that I watched just to see how magnificent the colors would be from one moment to the next with the sunlight hitting the cloud edges. Everyone talks about the green Northwest and its evergreens and naturescapes, but no one mentions that because we have differences of elevations and lots of cloud formations (yes, they talk a lot about the rain too), we have the most amazing miraculous sunsets.

In nature, there is no color control and your eyes accept the craziest of the craziest colors together. I have come to terms that God created nature in full Technicolor so we would let go of our judgment.

You can come to understand volumes about yourself when you ask what these colors mean to you and to those around you. After all when you look outside you have seen them in hundreds of variations. Everyone can understand as long as you ask the right

In nature, there is no color control and your eyes accept the craziest of the craziest colors together. I have come to terms that God created nature in full Technicolor so we would let go of our judgment.

questions. And the questions are: how does this make you feel, and why.

I met with a couple not long ago who were trying to work out their color differences. Somehow he couldn't see the beauty in her choices of combining lots of plaid and floral patterns and she couldn't understand his indecisive nature towards color. After all, couldn't he see how amazing these colors were together? This was the heyday of chintz, Waverly, and wallpaper. Lots of color in lots of patterns.

Every time they went shopping, they walked out without a purchase. She had had it with him and happened to be talking to a friend about it who said she had the perfect solution to save the marriage and gave her my number. She called me.

I knew I was walking into land mines and I was not sure who was not asking the right questions. So I started to help them by flashing pictures in front of them like a hot potato game where they only had a second to respond, hot or not to what they liked and disliked.

Colors, like features, follow the changes of the emotions.

~ Pablo Picasso

I put together piles of pictures that were his, hers, and both. Think of this as a color "hot potato" game. In looking through each pile for color clues, his had a ton of white images. When I noticed his pile was full of white pictures, they both looked surprised since he was not a guy who seemed to like white or see it as a contemporary influence in his life.

I asked if he liked white, and he said not really. I asked if he grew up with white, and he said not really. I said that it must have a meaning for him of cleanliness, newness, or commitment. His wife loudly and instantly shouted out (the way only a wife can) that his mother was a "junk" collector and that he had grown up in a house where only one person could walk down the hall because of all the stuff in the hallway. He absolutely, positively grew up to hate chaos.

He didn't know what to buy because the thought of having clutter, let alone color clutter, paralyzed him. Alas, white meant "order and peace" to him, and his wife's choices for colors in patterns were like an overwhelming crazy quilt to him. Seeing all those colors mixed together like wild animals made him, well, crazy. It takes a nonjudgmental attitude towards color to get to the bottom of this fierce ownership through emotion.

Color has meaning even if you don't know it. It can be cultural, personal, emotional and, sometimes, simply irrational.

I quickly showed them how solid color around busy patterns, along with neutral backgrounds, would make things more organized for him. Color has meaning even if you don't know it. It can be cultural, personal, emotional and, sometimes, simply irrational.

Your Turn

Make your color list of red, orange, yellow, green, purple, and blue. Think on each one and be very honest about what they mean to you. An example would be — I think of white as fresh, but it means "new" to me as I think back to when I was a kid. My grandfather painted all the walls white as a start of the new year. To someone else, they might think of it as fresh also, but have it mean "impersonal" as when they had to live in apartments most of their childhood. Try this with each color and discover a few things about yourself. It will help you see color though memory.

"THAT COLOR WILL WORK"

THE REAL JOB IS TO LOOK GOOD

CLIENTS OFTEN EXCUSE FUNCTIONAL colors they have because they think that great color and functional color are mutually exclusive.

So they state the differences between great colors, the ones that they want you to stop and look at like a stop sign, or make things invisible so it all goes away like ignoring beige carpet. They will say ignore the blue couch because it is a hand-me-down, or don't look at the bathroom tile because the pink can't change but we love the burgundy leather couch.

The job of a color is a lot easier and sweeter if the colors look beautiful together and do not need explanation. After all, who wouldn't want to look at the indisputable beauty of color in everything we own like nature affords?

That old blue couch can be a worn cool color with orange red walls and navy pillows, just like the pink tile can become a light shade of red plum among the richer burgundies you love. Even the taupe chair color that isn't even a real color can support the other colors by being the perfect neutral.

If you plan to make color look good, it will outperform and work harder for you than you can imagine. And nothing can do a better job at this than wall color!

Sure, we can ignore a color next to a color we don't like. After a while, things in your home, closet, and even in your own life become invisible to you so you lose the ability to discern what you love, want, or need. After reading this book, you should understand that personal color relationships can make it all sing, the good, the bad, and the ugly — through the power of its beauty!

My client had a home that she loved (*won't change*) and a fireplace she hated (*want to change*). Her husband loved it of course and the thought of painting the brick was absolutely out of the question and sacrilegious in his mind (*can't change*). Men have a way about how they feel about change. Generally speaking, they don't like it.

Their thought pattern ranges from *if it is*

> *After a while, things in your home, closet, and even in your own life become invisible to you so you lose the ability to discern what you love, want, or need.*

there, it's there for a reason so why change it, to *if you change it, what will replace it?* to *why replace it if it's not broken?* The brick was mid-century, orange-red with a little pink hint to it. That's the one you are thinking of. Lots of ranch style homes had it and still have it.

She hired me to make her a color palette that looked good with all the stuff she loved, but not the ugly brick. The pink elephant in the room was to be ignored no matter how much pink there was. She had picked the necessary color for the wall in the room with the brick fireplace. The purpose of the color was to make the brick look as harmless as possible.

Nothing really wrong there, just making ugly work. So when we got done with the palette, I had this amazing yellow called Devine Teak among all the other colors in the palette. She was in love with it and wanted it in her kitchen. Nice idea but I had other plans for it.

That's when I said that Devine Teak had to go with the brick on the living room walls. Shock, disbelief, alarm, doubt, fear and contempt. (Happens a lot in consulting.) She had just done

> I have played hell somewhat with the truthfulness of the colors.
>
> ~ Vincent Van Gogh

that room. There was a color already taking care of it

and she hated that brick. Why would we put the color she loved with the brick she hated?

How could I put the greatest color in the palette in a room that she lived to avoid? Easy. Wall color has a job and the main one is to make all the rest of the colors look good. So keeping that in mind, I wanted to make the brick color that was there look like it was a beautiful color. The neutral color had failed miserably at its task of making the brick look beautiful.

Once we put the Devine Teak in the room next to the brick, it embraced it. All this beautiful red came out and began to scream out loud, look at me, I am gorgeous! Gone was the orange, healthy was the red. It was the same yellow and red combo in the porcelain rooster in the kitchen, the same color combo in the bistro piece over the fireplace, and the same combo in her raffia woven Pier One placemats.

Her husband was feeling vindicated for having saved the brick fireplace from being painted or sheet-rocked and the wife was still in shock about how all the reds in her home were variations and shades of that particular brick. After the euphoria subsided, I did ask the husband why he liked that brick so much anyway.

Of course he had a story. He had grown

Wall color has a job and the main one is to make all the rest of the colors look good.

up in a home that had that brick. Later in life his parents split and sold the home. He loved the basement of that old house and it so happened, now that he thought about it, that the living room fireplace reminded him of it.

Funny, he didn't remember that till I prodded about the reasons why he loved the brick fireplace. His wife was so happy to know that bit of information that she actually kept repeating that story to everyone who came in as a testimony of how their family recovered from that loss! Victory and pleasure all through color.

We learn about the world through color. It helps us remember and differentiate between things, so much so that they can become nouns: "he saw red," adjectives: "blue in the face," and sometimes even verbs: "whiten your laundry." Consciously or subconsciously, we witness the beauty and the magic of flowers, seascapes, corals, leaves, sunsets, and sunrises and want to bring them into our everyday lives.

Particular colors convey a lot of day-to-day information. Red stop signs, blue light specials, yellow ribbons, and white flags. The red on the stop sign is there to make you stop. While you are looking at that stop sign, take a moment to notice how the streets look blue when wet or how next to the red there is a gorgeous green tree. It will make your journey so much more pleasant.

The same goes with the inside of your home. We choose dark bedding because the dog lies on the bed, white appliances because they go with the trim color, and black lamps because they are neutrals. We assign certain colors the job of being strictly functional.

Then there are the red chairs because you love red, the blue and yellow dishes because you love yellow and blue, or the sage green curtains in velvet because you don't even know why. It's all love when we choose color for beauty's sake.

If you plan all the colors to be right with each other, you will end up with beauty and function all at once. In my business, wall colors have the awesome job of making all the colors in the room look functionally beautiful.

Color has a job and as long as it is about how to make things meaningful and lovely, we might as well smell the roses with our eyes and make every color be beautiful.

Your Turn

Take what you think is the least likable color in your home so you can either change how it looks or get rid of it. How? Make a list with the colors you can't get rid of opposite the colors you can. Clean house first by getting rid of the colors you can and replace those things with colors you love.

When it comes to the ugly tile in the bathroom or the couch that you are waiting to replace when the kids go to college, pair them up with good color partners.

Think of the color that will come in and make the unloved color lighter or more colorful. For example, the taupe couch may look more purple next to a green wall or lighter up against a richer chocolate wall. Take it one color at a time. What are you willing to change, or not change? That is the question.

"EVERYBODY HAS TO LIKE IT"

EVERYONE WANTS TO UNDERSTAND IT

WHEN YOU GO PLACES, your eyes are like a camera snapping pictures all the time. Most of the time you can block out most of what you see until something snaps your head around and you have to stop and look at beautiful color. Like a sunset, a painting, or a garden, the six colors to the rainbow in color combinations that our eyes understand are recognized as perfect. Perfect beauty makes you stop. OK, so does ugly. This is when your eyes can't understand what they are seeing and colors are zooming in and out.

Beauty is in the eye of the beholder. A lot of people take this as a personal declaration that what they may think is beautiful, someone else may not. But if beauty is in the eye of the beholder, isn't the beholder looking for beauty in everything he or she sees? The key word here is beholder. Behold has two definitions:

> *To perceive by the visual faculty; see*
> *To perceive through use of the mental faculty; comprehend*

In my philosophy, it is about how everyone loves to be snapped back by beautiful color with their eyes and understand it with their intellect. This happens if they can see something put together and instantly comprehend it. That is when the beauty is truly in the eye of all beholders. Sharing that common experience is what makes it all so fantastic!

While color is personal, everyone sees it and therefore has to be a part of it, so it is not private.

In grade school when all the kids have their art projects hanging on the walls, we look at the pictures without contempt. We enjoy their interpretations, and most of the time, whatever the colors are, they seem to naturally make sense (somewhat) or offer us a certain reflection of what was going on in their brains; call it vision.

While color is personal, everyone sees it and therefore has to be a part of it, so it is not private.

Sure, some are better than others but what we love are the glimpses through their eyes and how their souls interpreted it — one subject with lots of different perspectives. That is what we want to see in colors that are put together. Everyone wants to see how you express these in your home with your own personality.

Color connects all of us through beauty. This is why art is never done in seclusion. Artists show their work to let everyone share their vision. This something that is communicated through art is at an emotional level and so here we go again with how we feel. As an artist, I hoped everyone who saw my work as a color consultant could see how I helped others experience color.

Because I believe in a philosophy that we are all able to recognize indisputable beauty in color, I knew those who saw the color palettes I built for my clients would react, understand, and enjoy them. Everyone else's eyes became my referral cards. The word of mouth spread among neighborhoods.

> I believe in a philosophy that we are all able to recognize indisputable beauty...

In one of these neighborhoods, the news of my expertise was going from household to household. I had one woman in a particular neighborhood call me because she had seen my work in several homes. They were a couple in their 60s and retired. The home was a buttercup yellow on the outside with a white wraparound porch. It had pinks and blues inside with white wood trim and older antiques. She was a quilter and she knew exactly what colors she liked. You could tell she still loved mauve and was proud of it. All she needed was to update her walls with colors that would make all of what she had collected look new again.

I was happy to help her and in the end came up with a wall color palette that made all of her colors look like she went out and bought them that day. By making relationships between what seem to be "pastel passé" colors with soft shades of current color, I made this home a Monet spring salad.

In short, with six colors to the rainbow, the pinks (red in the rainbow) and blues that were already there, combined with light greens and yellows, allowed her to broaden her color choices. Since she had reds and blues in their palest shades, they could now come in as bright color through richer reds, and deep periwinkles because the relationships were built around the new yellows and greens. They were thrilled and ready to paint.

Always curious, I asked where she had seen my work. She went on to say that she had been at a neighborhood party and had seen a home I had done she particularly liked. That seemed quite normal until I asked which home.

I was shocked to find out that the home she had seen was in complete opposite colors of what she liked. I knew the home well. It was perplexing. The home was full of everything new in rich neutrals, with black as a predominant accent. Having seen her home, I couldn't imagine what she could love about those colors.

When I asked her what her favorite room was, she said the one with the black piano, white fireplace, columns, and a black ceiling. This was the woman who loved those soft, pastel, feminine colors that literally defined her generation and here she was, admiring the personality and expression of a super cool thirty-something couple who were light years away from her cozy country feel.

She had seen beauty in someone else's colors and that had inspired her to find beauty within hers. Color is personal but not private. That means that while you think you are the only one who has the right to enjoy your colors, the fact is that everyone around you wants to as well.

Think of color like a favorite dinner dish you like to eat. The experience is so much better when you share it with others and everyone enjoys it.

As long as everyone has eyes, they will be able to recognize colors that are meaningful, purposeful, and personal without prejudice. We all have a need to understand and be comforted by what we see. That is why it is so important to find the colors you love and let them surround you in ways that are lovely to see.

Beautiful color combinations are like an instant snapshot, a painted memory, and a visual fragrance to remember things by. Hopefully, the kind of beauty we all want to recreate for ourselves will be expressed for all to enjoy!

Your Turn

Trust in the beauty you see by continually trying to understand what makes beautiful colors work together. Take the work of any artist that piques your curiosity and study his or her color relationships. Look for those repeated combinations in everything you see, from rugs to towels. How do they appear in your home?

"I COULDN'T SEE THE COLOR"

YOU DIDN'T WANT TO SEE IT

ONE OF MY CLIENTS was married to a color-blind man — not the type that women often tease about because they think men don't care about color or what they wear. Her husband's color blindness was real, so she loved to shower him with colors he could see. This couple actually understood what it meant to enjoy every color they could because in his world, some colors were missing. The home was full of bright color with lots of great purples, reds, bright oranges, and yellows. They had black and white checkerboard patterns along with splashes of black and white photography. Lots of geometric patterns and contrast.

The wood trim and cabinets were painted white, with oak floors and black countertops. The walls were a creamy light yellow. It was so non-intrusive, it looked like a tooth color. She had made some color mistakes by adding strong wall colors and wanted to stop herself before she ended up in more trouble. Having crazy-quilted herself with a red wall here and a purple wall there, she had also sponge painted a bathroom in bright gold before she quit. Here among the color rubble, she stood defeated, not knowing where to go next.

When I arrived, I had to look past all the colors and boil it down to one thing. They loved color so why not start there. The first thing I did was change the overall tooth color from their impersonal and bland creamy yellow that didn't relate to their love of color to Devine Fescue, a soft celery color, making a green relationship with all the colors. The soft green worked wonders in soothing the black (yellow would only energize it), pulling out the reds in the oak, contrasting the yellows and oranges (more color to see), and providing stronger companionship to all the reds and purples.

You see, the light creamy yellow was so anemic that it was like a buzzing instead of an effective color. As a result, I was able to give them more overall color and support the stronger colors they loved. The husband actually called me to let me know that even though he was color-blind and saw Devine Fescue as more of a gray, he could feel a difference in their home. It seemed the walls had simply relaxed by becoming a cooler color.

Then there are those who need help seeing a color

After you choose to not acknowledge the pink in the pink elephant, you then expect everyone to also ignore it.

because that is the last thing they want to do. They want to like it. They go as far as pretending their eyes don't see it. This is what most people will do after seeing a color that turns on them and ends up looking very different from what they thought. The recovery is slow because the denial is so deep. The fact is that after you choose to not acknowledge the pink in the pink elephant, you then expect everyone to also ignore it. Kind of the way a parent with a bratty child is able to shut it off and wants you to do the same.

I had a husband once buy a gift certificate for his wife. They wanted yellow. They were ready with pictures of every yellow thing they could find. I was very happy to help and began the conversation by telling them that if they were going to keep the mint green walls in the tall open entry, in combination with the orange hardwood floors throughout the home, we would have to then be specific about what kinds of colors would be good and yellow was not one of them.

They wanted a certain yellow but couldn't have it because it made the mint green blue and that would not be good with the orange floors because it would look like turquoise.

That is not mint green, it is sage green, they both kept saying over and over again to try to make the yellow work. So I took three greens and showed them the differences and theirs was the mint among them.

Silence, then the wife shouted to the husband, I told you it was mint green when we first saw it and you told me it wasn't. I hate mint green, I knew it was, and I let myself think it wasn't.

Because they had thought they were getting sage green and were shocked that they got mint, the mistake was too overwhelming to admit so she convinced herself it was not mint green.

He also turned out to be color-blind. When you know you want a color, the first thing to do is surround it with all the other colors you want. Soon enough you will see if you are heading in the right direction. Once we settled on the fact that the clients really loved yellow, we changed the green and all the colors they wanted came together effortlessly.

Had my clients looked at the first green next to all the yellows and reds they loved, that blue would have popped out from the mint and they couldn't have looked the other way.

When you know you want a color, the first thing to do is surround it with all the other colors you want. Soon enough you will see if you are heading in the right direction.

Blue flower, red thorns! Blue flower, red thorns! Blue flower, red thorns! Oh, this would be so much easier if I wasn't color-blind!

~ Donkey from *Shrek*

Not being able to trust your eyes is a scary thing. The lipstick that goes to orange, the shirt that makes your skin looked jaundiced, the bedspread that turned from purple to gray — we all have stories about how we just didn't see the color.

The six colors in the rainbow want to be in good company, so it is up to you to look for them so you can make good decisions.

Your Turn

Look. Look. Look around. I want this book to make you see what is in front of you, not look at pictures that you don't live in, with things you don't have. If you love color, then start with a color to make your relationships. How do you know? Simple, look at what you buy. Think about the furniture you have purchased or pieces of art, clothing, or rugs.

If what you buy are neutral colors, start with neutral relationships, making sure they work together, and then bring in colors that work with the neutrals. If you buy a lot of color, then neutrals may look dingy or dull. Your color relationships may be better off by starting with color and layering colors that carry their strength.

"THESE COLORS ARE SO ME"

YOU AND EVERYBODY ELSE

SUMMER ARRIVES AND THE patios are getting filled with flowers. Everyone has red geraniums, purple lavender, orange lilies, and yellow marigolds. The maple trees are in brilliant greens and reds. You are thrilled to be able to sit and enjoy your back yard and you're about to buy your umbrella cover for your patio set when you notice that the neighbor has red umbrellas and the other neighbor has green. All of a sudden, you are too late. You can't get the green or red like you were thinking you wanted because you are going to look like you're copying them.

Now what? Are you going to be stuck with some trend color you hate like that new lemon-lime, a cheerless generic neutral that looks gray or worse, or spend hours on the Internet looking for expensive alternatives. You feel like you have been cheated out of color. You have been left with the worst possibilities because you didn't get there first…you are stuck with the leftover colors.

You often see them in sales racks where they quietly get sold to people at a fraction of their original price. So now it is not even about the leftovers, now it's about cheap color! The ones nobody wanted or got to first.

Everyone is so concerned about their independence through color but how come no one worries about all the colors people share day in and day out, like flowers, a pair of black pants, or blue jeans? Somehow, while you are stressing over umbrella colors, you are able to block out of your mind the fact that you and all your neighbors all have the same flowers, shrubs, and outdoor grills.

Look around and see that we all share the six colors we claim to be ours! So often when I have clients who want a color and end up with one that is similar to their neighbors', they panic. I can't; she will think I copied her. Don't settle for some leftover color you really dislike.

With six colors to live by, everybody wants them, so we think it is a race to get there first. We somehow know that if we own that color first, it becomes ours. Once that happens everyone else will know it is yours and therefore off limits.

It's funny because when we are kids, we don't mind when we all want the same red popsicles. The top colors kids love in popsicles are red, purple, and green! With the younger generations you can add blue as a top candy color! So when the bags of popsicles or hard candy rip open and kids dive to get their favorites, the unwanted colors are the ones that are left for those who were a little too late.

Everyone is so happy to get their favorite color and having it be everyone else's favorite makes it even better. At this point sharing the same color is exciting.

My youngest daughter was once commenting on how kids who wore all black thought of themselves as making a statement, standing out in society and being different. I said to her that it was the same approach used in Catholic or prep schools by requiring the same color uniform.

When kids all wear black, this makes them all look the same, where their personalities, quirks and humor, taste, heritage, and creativity can't be discerned. So how are they standing out? They aren't. They want to look and be the same as everyone — just in a smaller group — and their idea of identity recognizes the color

Color can keep us from feeling lonely and make us feel like members of a community. I call this Color Clubbing.

black. This is how kids like it. To be in the group!

Color can keep us from feeling lonely and make us feel like members of a community. I call this Color Clubbing. We see it in sports teams with color used to symbolize their pack. Fans can wear their colors and feel like one of them, identify with them. When we get older, we want to have our individuality shine through, but there are always circumstances where we want to share the same colors.

There is nothing like how our red, white and blue Fourth of July declares our union and our independence all at once as a country. Outside our homes, we are happy to see our neighbors repeat this same trio of color, from flags, to flowers to desserts. Yet when it comes to certain things, we do not want to be in a Color Club. We want to get to the colors first and stake a claim. We love those colors and we want them all to ourselves.

You have been there. You walk into a home where the owners are friendly and warm. They greet you with open arms; offer you food, drinks, and anything you want — except the name of their wall color. That's right!! You begin to tell them how much you love it and how you would want to have it. Somehow they don't remember the color name. It is either a custom color they slaved over or has a number that does not come to mind. Sometimes this is just an excuse because they don't want you to have it. Simple. It's theirs. That's right. They don't want it in your home but they don't mind sharing the Cobb salad recipe.

Let say you haven't experienced this about a wall color, but I know you have with clothing. I was chatting with a very interesting man in San Francisco about this very subject. He couldn't believe that some people were that catty about wall color. So I said what about clothing? I'm sure you have been asked where you got a shirt or a pair of pants.

He said when he didn't want to tell someone about the source of the item in question, he would say he got it in New York. That's like saying, maybe Uganda or Guam. Conversation over.

I once loved these white boots a woman was wearing in a Minneapolis restaurant. They were so unique that I had to ask where she had gotten them; she said they were a gift...that was it. A gift, that's it? No more information, no let me tell you the brand or designer, simply...a gift. Didn't she know that if I had them I would wear them with different things? She wanted to be the only

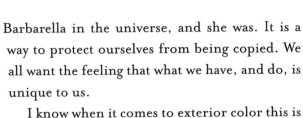

Barbarella in the universe, and she was. It is a way to protect ourselves from being copied. We all want the feeling that what we have, and do, is unique to us.

I know when it comes to exterior color this is a big problem. If green is what you were thinking of for the outside of your home and two neighbors beat you to it, now what? Let's face it, this often is what happens because there are only so many colors you are willing to risk putting outside on your home. Well, that happened in my old neighborhood. Around the same time, two neighbors painted using a sage green with off-white trim.

It was difficult at first because everyone who drove by compared the greens constantly. They were so similar that one made the other look slightly off. Then about six months later, one of the homes painted its door purple and voilà — all of a sudden, one house looked unique and totally apart from the other.

The purple made her red flowers in the front look vibrant; her green became smokier and her trim crisper.

The other home didn't have to change a thing. It now looked different because its own details such as a white wrought iron fence and cool gray rock stood out.

You are unique and different and your style will reflect it through your own color mix. Make the colors you love work with what you have and mix them with other colors to make your environment personal.

Nowhere do you see the same colors over again and again yet in so many individual color combinations than in the city of San Francisco. It is almost as if color is a birthright! Colors shake and bake in ways that make everyone notice the diversity. One color will be woven throughout many homes in many ways.

The influences of the Victorian era and their "painted ladies," along with a thriving artistic and business community culminate in a state of the union that declares unity and independence all at once. The best of both worlds. As with all colors, it is how you use them that makes them yours.

That red umbrella will have a different look with white patio furniture, pink flowers, and blue cushions vs. black wrought iron with gold tablecloths, chocolate cushions, and yellow roses. Whatever the color you need or want, get it and just make it personal by surrounding it with different combinations.

In the end, the fact that there are six

colors makes it impossible to create a secret society, one where you are the only member. The problem is that we fear someone else calling us "copycat." Not to worry. It is not a sign of lack of creativity or a homogeneous tendency; it is a sign of wanting the world to be more beautiful and being real about what you have to work with.

Your Turn

You are unique and different and your style will reflect it through your own color mix. Think of how you want to make your colors into a personal combination. You don't need to stick to colors you already have. Experiment! What is the dominant color that makes it so you? Try at least ten other colors that might go with it. Force yourself. If it is light blue, can you think of it with chocolate, cream, yellow, green, red, orange, coffee, white, black, or gray?

Once you pick one, start it again. Would you do the light blue and stone with pomegranate or navy? Coal or ice? Or would you do the light blue and pomegranate with terracotta or butter? Chocolate or brick? How about light blue and stone with ice, adding a bright green as in fern? That makes it different than putting it with cherry! Find samples of the color you love and surround it by other colors that make it more personal. You'll be stunned.

"You can't have those colors together"

They already are

Artists are the ones who really have tortured themselves throughout the ages to recreate the magic of colors that are so easily mixed in nature. Since there are six, believe me, we try to use every single combination we can think of because if not, we would paint, weave, or knit ourselves into a very boring corner.

There are no *don't's* about color as long as you combine them with the *do's*.

Outside color is totally out of our control. We see all kinds of beautiful color combinations that we would never think of and totally accept them as beautiful even if they are unusual. But inside our homes we are total control freaks. We want the colors to all match and stay in line.

No one worries about the green shrubs outside matching, but for the inside, they will take a swatch of the leaf on a pillow print and demand that green or else it won't

There are no don't's about color as long as you combine them with the do's.

work. The truth is that all the six colors can go together just like all of them can clash. Confusing?

The problem is that we seem to make a crazy rule about the colors themselves and we soon find ourselves limiting colors to this one with that one. My husband calls this the "I'm going to just go bald syndrome." He always says it is like saying just because you got a bad haircut, you are going to shave off your hair so it won't happen again. There are ways to make sure you or others can live with all kinds of great colors together and not just the ones you know can't go wrong. No need to throw the baby out with the bath water.

Maybe it is the way you saw the red on a shirt with a clashing purple pair of pants or some kid who picked out his own clothes combination that made you think that red and purple do not go together. The mustard chair at the neighbor's house, the guy wearing the black socks with Bermuda shorts — we have enough examples of bad color combinations to only want safety. Yet it is not about the colors themselves.

That mustard chair just needs the rich red pillows, a cream couch, butter walls, and blue paintings to all of a sudden be a warm Tuscany Gold antique! And what about the black socks and those Bermuda shorts, they'd better be with a bright yellow and black t-shirt ensemble. Just because you got into a car accident does not mean you should never drive on a road again.

Red and purple do go together and you see them in sunlight, in desert sands, and woven in cloth. There is a right yellow for each red, green, orange, purple, and blue, a right red for each yellow and so on. It is the way light works — by blending colors together with one another. That is why in nature you see so many variations.

Most people live in a world of pairs; you know, the blue-and-yellow or the red-and-green syndrome. So if you have a predominantly red and green home and I say I want to give you purple, the fear of clashing is palatable.

Yet, there is always a perfect purple that makes that red redder, the green cooler, and the other colors like the pinks in a pillow or the purple-blues in a vase previously drowned by the dominance of red and green look even better. This of course allows the great golds to follow behind with a now broader assortment of reds and greens.

I had a client who had all these blue and white collections of china patterns, plus

> There is a right yellow for each red, green, orange, purple, and blue, a right red for each yellow and so on. It is the way light works — by blending colors together with one another.

white walls, crown moldings, and boxed-ceilings, together with French country themes and lots and lots of pattern. This was the land of blue and white and the yellows, reds, and greens in the rest of her things were incidentals. If she ever bought color, it was the blue and white she saw first regardless of how they mixed with the reds, purples, oranges, greens, pinks, and/or neutrals.

She was looking forward to having the perfect blue accent wall to go with her china. I started with changing all the white walls to a yellow neutral that would complement all the blue and create contrast with the white. We needed to get out of the cloud we were in. We wanted to stay on the lightweight side, so we decided between Devine Custard and Devine Shell.

These two highlights of yellow color would complement the blue, making it bluer while becoming a shadow to the white, contrasting with it. We settled on Devine Shell. Now we needed the accent we were looking for and it was not going to be blue. It was going to be *red*. She was beside herself.

She believed she had no reason to have red walls. She didn't have anything in the house with red. She was going to end up looking like an American flag (bad haircut, shaved head), she said. Well, if I didn't do it, she was going to end up in a deep ocean where she wouldn't see anything but chunks of white floating on the surface.

The fact was that the blues and whites were so over-powering that adding more of them would actually make them disappear. Your eyes could take in only so much, so the other colors like the red, greens, and yellows of the accessories and wood were going to become spotty and distracting. It wasn't a blue and white world! She had orange floors to deal with and red and yellow roosters along with French bistro scenes. So I said, "We are doing the walls *red*."

What happened after that was a great relief. The red walls suddenly connected all the other colors she had that supported the lead cast of blues and whites. Devine Sangria had just the right amount of grit to appear smoky, unlike "American flag red."

Her fear of ending up like an American flag was gone. In her mind she was stuck in a blue and white world and if she added any other color, it would clash. The fact is that she didn't have just blue and white. Lots of blues and whites come mixed in with lots of other colors and she owned quite a few mixes throughout her house.

Now with the red, people came in and thought her collection was twice as large. Did you get new furniture? Is that a new vase? Did the floors get refinished? She found herself looking at the combinations of colors she had instinctually bought, marveling at all the colors. Most importantly, her blues just wowed the crowd even more.

This is what happens when you think past pairs.

All of a sudden you discover colors in the room that are magnificent and you would have otherwise missed them. Your eyes want to see all the colors. They want to have the same out-of-control feeling they have outside, because it is more exciting, more fun, and ultimately more satisfying! So what if red and blue are on a flag; does that mean you have to go bald!

When you have a color you love, you can surround it by all other colors as long as they have affinity and this allows you to have endless surprising combinations as opposed to staying with safe pairs.

Artists live for this thrill. We have already seen that thrill in multiple combinations of purples and reds, blues, yellows, oranges, and greens in hundreds of paintings, sculpture, and crafts. We have seen quilts that leave us breathless with complex color. All to say that nature has taught us that color gives freely of itself and the more you have, the more you will see.

Color is a safe out-of-control experience to have and that is what makes it perfect.

Color is a safe out-of-control experience to have and that is what makes it perfect.

Your Turn

Take the Devine Color palette. (I'm prejudiced.) Find at least one color from each color page and combine it with a selection from each of the neutral pages. It would be similar to what you would wear as a shirt with a pair of pants.

Take that color in your mind to an art museum and look for it in all the art pieces. Soon you will find there is a red for every color in the rainbow and so on. If it's a green you want, it is green you can have as long as it is the green that goes with the rest of the colors, just as the right shirt to the pair of pants.

Sure you can put together red and green and have it look like Christmas. But think about deep wines with hunter greens, earthy greens with spicy reds, silver greens with cherry reds, khaki greens with coral red. You can have those colors together if you make them relate because if you don't, you will find your colors clashing like a bad outfit down the red carpet.

"THAT COLOR WILL BE TOO DARK"

OF COURSE IT WILL UNLESS YOU TURN ON THE LIGHT

LET ME SHED LIGHT on this matter. Color does not produce light. It is a reflection of light and therefore needs light to be seen. People paint a room white if it lacks light because they want the room to appear light. Actually, to have it light, they need to turn on the lights.

Sure, one of the reasons I did this whole "Color Therapy from the Northwest" was because we were a little light-deprived, and as a result, this made us cranky sometimes. It is not only the cloudy or partially cloudy nine months out of the year that cuts back on sunlight, it is our soil, so rich that every shrub grows to be a tree and we have a ton of trees blocking light. We love our trees and this leaves us a little in the dark inside. I created these amazing colors that I felt had great purpose and a relationship to light so they would go with what we all had in our lives.

> People paint a room white if it lacks light because they want the room to appear light. Actually, to have it light, they need to turn on the lights.

So when our paint partner was looking to hook up with a manufacturer on the East Coast to bring this great concept to everyone's lifestyle, their marketing team felt that the concept was strong but didn't understand why they would need to "import" color therapy *from* the Northwest *to* the East Coast. They knew Colonial, Historical, Cottage, Cape Cod, but Northwest?

Here in the Northwest we are more like pioneers in our approach to style. Our style is all about lifestyle — the one we experience through our great Northwest cuisine, our micro brews and world-class wines, our coffees and teas and great outdoor sports such as biking, windsurfing, hiking, skiing, golfing. We spend most of those rainy days creating things that are representative of our lifestyle.

For me, it was all about indoor color. The inspiration of all the names of my colors came from the amazing lifestyle the Northwest offers. This is why I have colors like Devine Cabernet, Bordeaux, and Ale. When you look at them, you want to live them.

My rainbow is inside Cool Grasses and Evergreens, Valley Vineyards and Spices, Natural Blondes, Desert Lights, Silver Skies, and Ocean Tide Pools. My neutrals are in Pebbles and Creams, Espresso Blends, and Pacific

Trail Mix. I am among many entrepreneurs who have translated our lifestyles into business.

John Hampton said, "Art is good business." And to me, so is color.

They say it takes three years to get used to the rain, and then you love our mild seasons and cozy weather. A lot of people from California have sacrificed a little bit of sun for an amazing lifestyle.

This typical couple from this very common circumstance had just made the move into a new home, a new life, and brand new furniture for their new Northwest lifestyle. They had just moved to Oregon from California and had spent their first winter here. The dull gray skies during winter had made their home look dull and gray. They knew that their white walls looked cold so felt they had to do something about the color. They thought that by making all the colors light, it would be bright. Wrong assumption.

They thought that by making all the colors light, it would be bright. Wrong assumption.

This was very typical of what I first encountered as a color consultant. My clients had lived with "builder white" and were ready for color — as long as it was more white. They were afraid that anything else would be dark and make their home even darker when it was already dark enough because of the clouds and shrubs. So they were cranky.

When suburbs exploded here in the eighties, the builder market boomed and the suburbs were blanketed with builder white. It was a clean slate, a blank canvas that everyone could start with and most of all it was light. The problem is that when you start filling up a white canvas without covering all of it, it can look like you missed painting part of the picture.

The husband was adamant about his office being some shade of white. I said it was not a problem as long as he recognized that it was not really ever going to be white; it was always going to look gray. What did I mean by that? Well if you looked at this office, it was not really white; it was about 30% gray. The small window in the den was really making the white walls look gray. There was not enough light in the room for it ever to be white. Well, he was afraid it would be too dark with any other color, he said. So the question became what color could make a light-deprived room lighter, other than white?

What do you think? I think, how much whiter than white can you get? Where there is little light, there is a lot of gray and that is what shows up on white walls. Your options are very simple. It is rich color that your eyes can see through little light. You need a favorite color that won't remind you of how much gray there is but how much you love that color. How dark a color is

The most important thing in light-deprived spaces is to have contrast between light and dark colors, because you're not going to be able to see anything if all the colors are the same value of light or dark.

has to do with it being relative to how dark or light the other colors around are. Color does not live in isolation so it is very clear that in these relationships, color can be looked at almost like a gray scale where if 1 was white and 10 was black, all the numbers in between can fluctuate due to the relevance of what is around.

The most important thing in light-deprived spaces is to have contrast between light and dark colors, because you're not going to be able to see anything if all the colors are the same value of light or dark. That is why you need evil to see good.

If all the colors are too dark, you can't see. If they are too light, you can't see anything either. Call it the yin & yang or the antagonist and protagonist; having opposites only sharpens differences and lets you see which side you are on! Let me give you a little tip, if 1 is white, and 10 is black, try going around your room to see what kind of contrast you have going on between things. Too many 5's, drab! Too many 2's with 7's, severe.

The way to see light colors in low-light rooms is to put darker ones next to them so you see contrast.

The way to see light colors in low-light rooms is to put darker ones next to them so you see contrast. This den had light cherry furniture, so we ended up contrasting the cherry wood with white Devine Icing moldings and the walls with Devine Almond, a soft, medium blue-green that contrasted with the warmth of the wood. All of a sudden the red popped out of the cherry because the blue-greens were creating contrast. The cherry was a 6 and the Devine Almond a 4. The white trim being a 1 was a crisp focus that you could even see if the lights were off!

> All colors will agree in the dark.
>
> ~ Sir Francis Bacon

It was his favorite room and he hung up all these beautiful coastal prints that made him feel right at home. Go ahead and make your own light in a room with color. You can make a room clean up its dirty cast with good contrast, bright rich color, and the right color partners. If you just want more light, call the electrician.

All those California clients, or out-of-town transplants like them, picked up the phone and told their friends in other parts of the country, and soon Devine Color was not just "Color Therapy *for* the Northwest," it became "Color Therapy *from* the Northwest." The word of mouth spread like wildfire.

What did everyone have in common? This color line had become an amazing solution during a time of change. After all, when colors sing your environment becomes the perfect place to make everyone feel at home.

The National Trainer for Dacor appliances is an Oregon transplant. Dacor at the time was in the process of moving from Pasadena and building their brand new 45,000-square-foot facility in Diamond Bar, California. He told their designer to stop the presses; they had to have Devine Color. They flew me to California and the designer and I worked on a full color palette for their offices and their showroom.

When I flew back for an event, I couldn't believe my eyes how amazing Devine colors looked in California light! Colors like Devine Steamer, a deep pond blue-green that looked sulky and sexy in our winter light looked cool and refreshing in the bright sunlight. But most of all, regardless of the type of light, they had a place among all the other colors that made the wood tones look richer, the fabrics more colorful, and the space full of ambiance.

Devine Color became a color solution for all types of light in all types of climates. I had been so diligent at developing color with the Northwest lifestyle that the natural rich hues of the colors, their connection to wood, and the way the paint finishes reflected color made them applicable everywhere. These colors had adaptability to their environment that was uncanny.

When you hear Historical, Cape Cod, Southwestern, or Colonial colors, everyone instantly gets the picture. "Color Therapy from the Northwest" offered the consumer a kind of independent spirit of the Northwest — where you can live in your own skin.

When you see other "designer" color palettes out there, you will see their theme or spokesperson. After all, you know that Martha Stewart colors look like Martha and Ralph Lauren colors look like his brand, but when you see Devine colors, you won't see me or even think of the Northwest. You will see yourself living in them.

Your Turn

When you cannot tell if a color is going to be too light or too dark in a room, give all of the colors a number. Start with looking around your room and calling the lightest color a 1. Then call the darkest color 10. Call all the other things the numbers between. So what do you have? Do you have a lot of 1's? Then you need more 4's or 5's. More like all 4's? Get some 8's or 2's in there. No matter how much light you have, it is all about the contrast between the colors. Think of how a dimmer in the room would change all the light and dark colors together.

So your oak floors are a 5, your cherry cabinets are a 7, your granite countertops are a 4. This will tell you right away how light or dark your walls should be, such as a 3 for a lighter feel or an 8 for rich drama.

"I can't find the color I'm looking for"

You are not looking

There are hundreds of neglected living rooms that are like color leftovers in the fridge — nobody wants to have them. You can recall walking by the old mauve and blue furniture, the teal, gold, and burgundy drapes or the cream on cream carpet, sofa, and window treatments, all amazing time capsules defined by trend color combinations.

Meanwhile there are the new freshly served colors in the family room that only make the living room colors and the family room colors look like feuding families. This puts a cramp in the colors we love and makes us feel like we have no options or recourse other than surrender to have a home half-done in colors with one foot in what was and the other in what is.

One of my favorite places ever was a client's home in the Northwest area of Portland. As soon as I walked in I thought

> Twenty minutes ago I was hot and now I'm just a cautionary tale.
>
> ~ Jerry Maguire from *Jerry Maguire*

to myself, this is magic. She was standing firm with both feet in the now. Nothing looked like a leftover dish.

The condo was small, yet cramped, with colors that seemed timeless, not as in a time capsule, but outside of itself. A time capsule would have seemed like whatever trend was in vogue at that time. It would be earmarked by specific color combinations that defined the decade, trend, or style of the time. I've been to a few of those. I think of them often as the Gracelands of suburbia.

But you could have walked into this place any time within the last 20 years and not know what year it was. There were contemporary art pieces with English antiques, shag rugs with teak shelves and a Pottery Barn couch. Deco mirrors, accessories, hand-me-downs, and lots of personal treasures were all mixed together in a color bouquet that was perfect. How did she do it?

Well, as I looked around, it seemed she never denied herself anything she truly loved and recognized that only color could make the relationship between the things she loved work. So she carefully arranged colors to have meaning and relationships, regardless of when they were bought. It was 1800 square feet full of treasures.

It is not that she had
every color in the rainbow.
It is that she had the
colors she loved surrounded
by colors that made them
even more perfect.

It is not that she had every color in the rainbow. It is that she had the colors she loved surrounded by colors that made them even more perfect.

Anyone walking into this home could be visually thrilled by color, like a painting of indisputable beauty. Believe me there is so much out there to collect, you *do* have enough color! Most people are very consistent about what they like and it is not that hard to see, once you connect your color dots. That is a big part of my job when I color consult. I want to find out what you love. This is what makes your world inside your door perfect.

When it comes to color, you have six that range from light to dark and cross over into different combinations to create a cast of thousands. Each of the six colors in the rainbow will pair up and become complements to create harmony or work in opposition to one another creating contrast. So if you look closely, they are all there.

I believe that this is why flea markets, vintage clothing, and antique stores are all the rage. Trends show that the resale business is a new untapped market soon to explode with specialty "thrift boutiques" opening everywhere. They will help meet the retro demand for old colors and styles that are no longer manufactured and influence new retailers to recreate the old looks as well. The colors you loved before and love now weave in and out of time, allowing you to become a bounty hunter for individual style. If you don't find what you're seeking, you can always find it in what was before.

I had a client tell me she loved yellow. She was having problems making all the new yellow things she had gotten work with her other stuff. As we kept looking at her collections, both old and new, it was evident she liked orange. She was very surprised. While she thought she liked yellow, her yellows were red-yellows not yellow-reds.

It was evident by the reds and greens she chose to go with them. The reds were orange, the greens were more olive and earthy. The newer yellows in the market had green in them that made her other greens look muddy and dirty. Alas, the manufacturing industry had changed her yellows without her even knowing it.

> All colors are the friends of their neighbors and the lovers of their opposites.
>
> ~ Marc Chagall

So we ended up with staying away from yellow walls, which were only going to create more disparity between the two yellow directions. We needed something on the walls that went with warm reds and neutrals so that all the yellows, reds, and greens worked as shades of one

> *The six colors of the rainbow can work miracles as backgrounds that make all you own look like you placed them inside a beautiful masterpiece.*

another. This made them seem like they were purchased just yesterday. What do your collections look like? Are the colors you love evident?

The reality is that it is the same six colors being revisited over and over again in different combinations. Avocado is now wasabi, harvest gold is now Tuscany. These six colors, whether in mauve, dusty rose, or pale blush, will continue to find new versions of themselves and new meaning in our minds. Wall color is the one place where you can fill in the blanks with colors when all the pieces need to get pulled together. The six colors of the rainbow can work miracles as backgrounds that make all you own look like you placed them inside a beautiful masterpiece. And when you can't find it, you can always paint it.

Your Turn

Think of one strong color that has come in and out of your life, one you've hung onto no matter what, and see how it is sprinkled throughout the things you own now. What color was it called originally? Pink, orchid? What is it called now? Rose, blush, cameo? Some Devine choices would be Devine Berries, Devine Glow, or Devine Pebble.

"I AM AFRAID OF COLOR"

YOU ARE AFRAID OF MAKING A WRONG DECISION

NOBODY IS AFRAID OF color. You see it every day coming at you in all forms, shapes, and sizes without flinching. You multitask so well with it and are fully in control of what you see; you have even learned to ignore it altogether. So, why do I hear so often, *I'm afraid of color, my husband is afraid of color, my friend is frozen with fear about color,* but I never hear *my children are afraid of color*?

Kids do not associate emotional needs with color; they associate *pleasure* with it and that takes care of lots of needs!

We are all afraid of making decisions that are not correct. Imperfect decisions lead to consequences where you could be wrong. If you are wrong, that makes you foolish, and being foolish makes all of us very afraid. When we are foolish about color, the whole world sees it so you are doubly afraid.

Kids do not associate emotional needs with color; they associate pleasure with it and that takes care of lots of needs!

The truth is always simple. The fear comes from pain, risk, or embarrassment of our own expectations. With color, you are the person responsible for the decision. This makes you master and commander of the ship, so if it sinks, it is your fault.

So let's take the sources of fear one at a time. Pain. You know the feeling. You see a pretty little color that you think will be so bright and cheerful you can't wait to paint it in the room. It goes on every wall and by the end of the week every time you are in that room your headaches won't go away. You feel nauseous, and as a matter of fact, your eyes hurt. The pain of repainting stays with you forever!

Then there is risk. The pitfalls of risk in color are many. The risk of losing the money you spent on buying that color, the risk of having to live with that color once you commit and hating it, the risk of the color taking over and having to buy more colors to make it work. Spending money on gas trips back and forth, and of course time is money.

Finally embarrassment. This is the one that really paralyzes us. We have all been there. Even if we can clearly see what is in front of us, we fail to choose the right color. How could you not have seen how bad that color was? How can someone say it looked like something out of a bowl of pea soup? You can't be embarrassed if there is no one around, so you know that embarrassment comes from interactions with how other people's you act and what you do.

A good friend tried a new place to have her hair done. When she called me, she said with a voice of disbelief, "I look like I'm on fire." A natural blonde from a bottle with green eyes, she was mortified at her now orange hair. She wasn't quite sure what had happened but all she knows is that she was at the grocery store when a sweet senior citizen had let her know that she loved her hair color because it matched the color of the gladiolas she was buying. They were orange.

We all want to have our friends, peers, and family like us or, at best, understand us. But not because we look like a gladiola.

Color, while personal, is not private and that means that it is the subject of scrutiny and judgment. It is OK to not

Color, while personal, is not private and that means that it is the subject of scrutiny and judgment. It is OK to not care what others think, but when we have been fooled by color mistakes, our confidence dwindles to nothing, and we doubt our abilities about our color knowledge and expertise.

care what others think, but when we have been fooled by color mistakes, our confidence dwindles to nothing, and we doubt our abilities about our color knowledge and expertise.

Your Turn

In a perfect world, there would be no fear. As a matter of fact it is well known that love casts away all fear. Color can help you find both tranquility and excitement by knowing which ones you love, knowing that they all look best when put together well and that others want to have the great thrill of seeing them. Your discovery can lead to a lifelong love affair with color. Make a list of things you've decided not to buy because of your fear of their color — things such as a sunflower-orange sofa, a raspberry-flavored dress, or a bright lemon yellow pair of golfing pants.

The Truth Behind What We See:
The Rainbow

The facts are simple but the way we see is complicated. Because seeing color is one of the five senses, it is all about the sensation you get from color, much like when you smell fragrance, taste wine, dance to music, or touch skin.

RED

WHEN TO USE RED and when not to use red? There are no rules, but red works magic at igniting every single color in the rainbow. It is able to pair up with everyone so why is everyone afraid of red? Because they think red will get all the attention when in fact, it is one of the colors that plays so well with others, it often gets denied.

One of my clients had just had her last kid leave home so she was facing a life of caring only for herself. She was ready for color excitement in her life but not red. Yet red was the answer for many reasons she would later understand.

She didn't feel like a red person and felt she had no red in her home. Yet when I told her that we would have to do red in the room, she almost passed out. The excitement soon became a personal terrifying scary ride! Give me another color. There was no other. Even though she bought a lot of greens and yellows there was always red in the mix. Therefore that's what made the colors she loved pop! OK, that made some sense because she couldn't deny it.

How could she have painted herself into a red corner she kept wondering? I said to her you can always do a neutral like Devine Macadamia or Filbert, but the bottom line is if you are serious about living with color, that color is red.

Those who turn themselves over to the exuberance of red are fully rewarded by what the color offers, great celebration.

ORANGE

WHO CAN DENY THAT the credit given to stunning sunsets falls on orange, which makes all the other blue, purple colors go crazy.

Santa Fe is where you would see orange in color relationships that have no boundaries because all you have to do is look outside and see the glory. Sunlight is a filter that blankets everything, so you see it in the way orange mutates on the desert and in the sky with rich blues, purples, and lavenders; sage and eucalyptus greens; bright reds, deep reds, dark blues, blue greens, turquoise blues, light yellows, and green gold. You get the picture.

These colors are also reflected in galleries, with selections ranging from jewelry to pottery to canvas. This time the filter of sunlight becomes the artist who blankets his or her vision over all the colors to make them connect. Once you see orange used as a great side dish to the all the different partners, you won't think of it belonging to a "southwest style" as much as belonging to our world.

In my business, many homes ended up with orange and the home owners don't even know it. Oak is orange, believe it or not. As a matter of fact, when I point this out as a color that has to be considered because of all the existing *oak* floors, it is perplexing how so many have lived with orange without ever considering it orange. They acknowledge the yellow tones in the wood but forget that all the red mixed in makes it orange. This was one of the single most important things I addressed with Devine Color; it was created to be a counterpart to the colors in wood.

YELLOW

YELLOW IS NEVER OUT of style. It becomes a light, bright kind of color that you can squeeze in anywhere to make things bright and light. Yellow on walls is an instant promise of warmth, friendliness, and a cup of cheer. At least, that is what we hope for.

Everyone wants yellow. They want that warm, friendly feel and are willing to go the extra mile of finding the magical yellow that will do it. Maybe it's our European influences, such as Italian and French yellows that have brought new excitement to traditional decor. Whatever the reason, yellow has become an instant solution to creating warmth.

Most of us do not realize how many yellow things we live with. What they can't see is that there is yellow in their oak floors, in their maple cabinets, in granite or fireplace brick. There is already enough yellow. Let some other color have the job of being warm for a while.

Often I get hired by designers who bring me into their projects as they would a lighting specialist. One particular designer always started with "Gretchen, what do you think? I was thinking of a warm, lemon, Tuscan, golden, creamy, buttery, you-name-it yellow" for every project she had. The problem was that everything the designer loved didn't love yellow.

That's right. She always picked surfaces with red undertones that would turn pink instantly once you placed any yellow next to them. She wanted the ambiance of yellow and thought of it mostly like a warm cast. In fact, it is a bright color that if paired up with the wrong partners can make all the other colors look overshadowed.

GREEN

WHEN IN DOUBT, DO green. Green is a color that assures us we know what we are doing. There are so many versions of green we have seen that we understand it like a well-known dish. Everyone knows that in nature the greens do not even have to match one other. We see every single shade, variation, and transition throughout the seasons, but with its abundance, it can become a little boring. It is not green's fault that it is the most common color in this world.

❧

Green will remain the anchor color on earth — the color that teaches us about transformation, adaptability, compatibility, and ultimately the abundance of beauty.

❧

Having green be such a part of our experience makes it all the more personal in regard to favoring one green over another. Certain ones stand out to us in the vast ocean of greens we see everyday and I believe there is a clear dividing line between the two kinds of "green" people. They love (because

no one really hates it) either the greens with blue or the greens with yellow. The chances are that the greens they choose say a lot about the rest of the colors they love. In every color story, there is a green for every season.

Green will remain the anchor color on earth — the color that teaches us about transformation, adaptability, compatibility, and ultimately the abundance of beauty.

BLUE

THERE ARE SOME WOMEN who refuse to have blue. But
while some women really dislike blue, others love it. I
never know which one I am going to get when I walk
through a front door. The funny thing about blue is that
while calming and peaceful, reliable and trustworthy, it
seems to produce a rebellious side effect in
some women.

Even if it fits perfectly in your palette, it
sometimes is a lot more than just about col-
or. It is all about how it makes us feel. Because
blue is so strong for your eyes, you can use it in
abundance or in small portions. In abundance,
paired up with oranges, purples, and reds, it
is the perfect balancing partner. Paired up
with yellows and whites it becomes an all-star,
and with greens and earth tones, it becomes a
mood-setting chameleon.

Everyone is born favoring blue due to its physical

hold on your vision. Those who remain faithful to blue as their favorite color like it so much that they never want to try anything else that they couldn't pair up with blue. They are the blue people. They do not like yellow tones in their green, they like blue-green. They do not like orange in their red, they like blue reds. They love purples because of blue. They like the right yellow only if it goes with blue and they can't imagine orange anywhere.

Blue can be fresh, peaceful, restful, and soothing. Too much of it can overwhelm your eyes, make you feel too calm, even slow down your blood pressure. For however much we love or hate it, one thing for certain, we can't avoid how strongly we feel about it.

PURPLE

WITH PURPLE IT IS either love or hate. You either love the color and want it on everything you buy or you hate the color and won't be able to stand a strand of it any-where. The decision about purple is made instantly. While people who *hate* purple will give you the many reasons why they hate it, people who *love* purple will never give a reason why they love it. They just do. They do not have to explain why and it is evident to them that you are the one who misunderstands the color.

I once had a client who I thought loved purple. It was a slam-dunk. This house was full of purple flavor. Their leather couch had red-plum tones and all their prints or accessories had purple and mauve written all over them. You get the picture. Purple was loud and clear!

So I went to work on a great purple palette paired up with other colors like greens, reds, and oranges. Everything was humming right along when the wife said to me she wanted a certain kind of yellow. This was a bright, beautiful, crisp yellow.

I said it was like they had invited these purple colors to the party and my job was to make it a great party, but the yellow she wanted was not welcomed. This is when a little minor detail about their lives popped up. It was all his ex-wife's stuff! Pandora's box blew wide open and it was his ex-wife's color that was shouting loud and clear.

This wife hated everything in the house and as a matter of fact, she went on to say she hated purple. The husband was shocked. He thought she liked the stuff. She didn't; she was only trying to compromise. Now that is love.

WHITE

WHILE YOUR EYES ARE amazing reading instruments of light, it is hard to read white. White reflects when it bounces back from solid objects, and just like it is hard to stare at a light bulb for a long time, it is hard to stare at white.

White wants to be relative to whatever is darker. White is like squeezing all the colors of the rainbow spectrum into a ball. As always, with neutrals, one to several of the six colors of the rainbow will always try to dominate, but with white, it is a very faint hello. This is why we have yellow whites, pink whites, green and purple whites, and orange and blue ones too.

The problem is that sometimes people use white not as a color but as a solution to dark, making white a less-than-perfect color choice. Your eyes want to have an easy experience at recognizing and under-standing color and they want to see white as a color, not as light pretending to be a color. But when you use a white background as light without any specific purpose, it disconnects all the colors around it and your eyes won't be able to stop looking at it. This is when white becomes distracting.

White-on-white schemes can be very beautiful and sophisticated; however, the focus is not the differences between the whites but the harmony among them so they all look as one.

Like white on teeth, snow, or clouds, light will reflect various shades of color but your eyes want to look at it as simply white because your brain has enough to think about. Having to stare at whites to see the almost invisible color differences between them is frankly exhausting.

I grew up with the meaning of white being the sign of new beginnings. Right before the holidays when my grandfather would paint the house white, this yearly ritual seemed to wash away all grievances of the past and be a fresh sparkling color to toast in the New Year. I will always love white as a color that brings freshness.

BLACK

WHY WOULD BLACK MAKE things more real? Because you need depth, black is what takes away the one-dimensional shallowness of color and plunges it into a different dimension.

Black is an icon. In fashion, no other color is used to such extent and variety. Black is associated with elegance, luxury, and of course the dark side. As color, black is used as a neutral. It is often said that something black should be in every room. It is perfect as the opposite of white or as sharp contrast to yellow or red and smooth along with blues and purples. Just like white has a function of being light, black has a function of erasing. It fills the space in the opposite way. I believe that the phrase "black goes with everything" exists because it erases itself.

> Without black, no color has any depth. But if you mix black with everything, suddenly there's shadow — no, not just shadow, but fullness. You've got to be willing to mix black into your palette if you want to create something that's real.
>
> ~ Amy Grant

The Truth
Behind Making the Rainbow Work

The Neutrals

THERE ARE COLORS IN nature that are so perfect they do not need to be seen. They are the colors that are perfect for places where you don't want to have color as much as the presence of it. Call it the spirit of color, or the soul. Neutrals are colors you want to feel rather than see. The feelings can be warm, cool, fresh, sultry, or sexy without the blue, red, orange, purple, yellow, or green jumping out. You can't have the whole house in a color that constantly wants your attention, and that is why the right neutral with just a hint of color can fill in lots of these gaps. Hallways, laundry rooms, kitchens with too much going on, bedrooms with leftover furniture or large ceilings can benefit from neutrals that do not outline, focus, or show off.

They are moody, vague, obscure, hazy, mild, shadowy, dusty, remote, and totally undetected. Whatever muted

> Neutrals are colors you want to feel rather than see.

color you use, its purpose should be one of harmonizing the environment and turning the volume down on all the other colors. This is why I always start with the perfect neutral so when we place colors in their right order, the neutral takes care of the rest of the walls that are left. The home never feels like it is partially neglected because it is full of colors that go with each other and neutrals that make it easy on the eyes. You live with neutrals right now that are simply taken for granted, such as oak, cherry, maple, marble, granites, and other hard surfaces.

> Whatever muted color you use, its purpose should be one of harmonizing the environment and turning the volume down on all the other colors.

I think of them like skin. Skin has different hues and different depths of color. It is the skin color that determines what kinds of red you can wear as well as determines if you can wear green or not. You remember the color hit *Color Me Beautiful*. This was a book that revolutionized the way women thought about color on their skin. It categorized everyone's skin colors into four different seasons: spring, summer, fall, and winter.

It actually made a lot of sense. If your skin tones were red, for example, that made you a summer or fall and there were colors that would make you look healthy or anemic. It had little fabric swatch palettes that women all over the country would walk around with to make sure that their skin looked great with all the rest of the colors. While it was all about the colors that looked good, it was the skin color that was the important factor. Your home should have a great skin color to begin to dress up.

The Brights

SHARP BRIGHT COLORS ON fabrics are fun, interesting, and attention-grabbing. We think of these colors as "the more the merrier," but they often end up becoming highly irritating when they are used too much. A little goes a long way, and as wall colors, they can be great fakes!

These are colors that you can see in dark rooms. Let me explain. Everyone wants a light color in a dark room because they think it makes the room lighter.

We have already discussed that color does not produce light and only reflects it. If there is no light, you can't see very well. Think of a dark room like being under sunglasses. For you to actually see a color, your choice would have to be several shades brighter because the dark lenses mute the brightness.

For example, I had a client once who had a room perfect for this fake, a basement children's playroom with one small window and really bad lighting. I used this wild, bright yellow in the room knowing the room's lack of light would produce the sunglasses effect. It ended up looking like the softest buttery spread on walls. It was perfect until they put in really good lighting, and then it looked like some place Big Bird would call home! Of course it did. The light with the bright yellow was blinding.

I congratulated her on her remodel and had her repaint with a light soft butter color, which is the color we would have done originally.

The Opposites

I HEAR THAT IT has been said when you can't match it, you have to clash it. Choosing a wall color that is not really present in the room yet embraces all the existing colors with it might be what the doctor ordered. Let's say you are stuck in the color pair syndrome and you have painted yourself into a corner where no other color can come in. You have seen the yellow and blue rooms where only yellows or blues will work. Sure, other colors might be in there somewhere, but there's no chance of seeing them. These colors are in small proportions or are so weakened by the strength of the color combinations that they are a faint cry in the room. Opposite colors are the perfect solutions to rooms that are stuck in that rut.

Opposite colors are the perfect solutions to rooms that are stuck in that rut.

You want to bring some hot orange or purple into this blue and yellow room. Then paint the walls **red**. Yes, I know that there is nothing red in the room right now but once the red is on the wall, you will see. This color clash can open up the palette where the blue and yellow are now related to the red instead of just each other. That is why purples and oranges can now enter the scene and have a place. All the colors will relate to the red. When you are stuck, bring in a color that will blow it all up and all colors that are there, plus the new ones you want, will land safely.

Drastic problems need drastic measures and this remedy is for those who want to take the plunge without having to buy everything new.

Final Thoughts
on Perfect Color Solutions

Beauty Is in the Eye of the Beholder
So Start Beholding...

As LONG AS YOU have eyes and a brain, you are all beholders. This means you all want to see and understand, and only then can you have beauty in the eye. This is why in nature, we all behold and understand all the color combinations with our eyes and our minds, and therefore we all agree on the beauty that we are beholding.

Remember: *Taupe, beige, and cream are not really colors because they are not in the rainbow.*

It should be as simple as remembering that everything is a color and that there is no taupe in the rainbow. The reason why things sometimes look neutral or without real color has to do with colors canceling each other out when they bounce off each other.

But if you look closely, a color will fight itself to the surface and claim its right. Oak wood has lots of yellow, red, and green tones but in the end, you can call it orange. The tan coat you

own is really a light khaki greenish yellow, making it a green-yellow when you wear a yellow sweater with it and yellow-green when you wear it with a red blouse.

If you surrender to the fact that taupe, beiges, browns, and gray colors are all really neutral forms of color that love to be with each other, your reality just got more exciting and interesting.

Remember: *You think it is about that color, but it is not.*

The sooner we realize it is about colors together we like and not just one color, the better decisions we will be able to make. Colors cannot be alone. Like people, no man (and no color) is an island.

We have seen it in so many couples. They bring the best or worst out in each other. Either way, we love being around the great couples and avoid the bad ones.

The troubled ones are in constant conflict while others bore themselves to death. Then one day you see half of the bad couple with a new partner. Suddenly the one who seemed so argumentative now seems very witty and the life of the party. The one who seemed so boring is now insightful and thoughtful.

I am not talking here about people; I am talking about color. But like people, those around them influence them. Opposites attract as long as they understand each other's needs. The color you love needs to allow all the colors you love.

The story often goes like this. A color begins to stand apart from everything else you thought you loved. At first you try to reason with it, compromise, and then you realize you made a mistake because having that color means not being able to have the colors you love around.

Colors that play well together stay together, they say, or at least I say.

You shouldn't purchase a color unless you know where you are going to put it. You buy color to put it in its place. Top or bottom, tie or socks, couch or drapes, walls or trim. There is a reason for not buying blue lipstick. It is not the right place for that color. This logical reasoning gets totally ignored, and nowhere is this more evident than in wall color.

Colors in other industries are assigned to objects. Some colors hold their position throughout time. For example, red lipstick lands on lips throughout the centuries because it creates a healthy look. Blue for denim is the American way. Black leather is a classic sexy staple.

However, with paint, people are under the impression that anything goes anywhere. Here is the question: If you were to buy a 400-square-foot couch, what color would it be? Now, the brain starts thinking. The color would have to look good that size, it would have to be placed correctly in the house, and the color would certainly have to have purpose. Wall color has the amazing responsibility of being the largest, biggest, and most important color in a room because of size. Not every color can go there. Great wall color for a room needs to be put in its place. And no matter what they say, size does matter.

Remember: *Not every color can be the best, greatest, attention-grabbing color.*

The red office, the yellow laundry room, and the green bathroom can't all scream for your attention. As you walk down the hall your head is turning every which way. The uncomfortable turning of the head caused by your eyes snagging glimpses of all these colors causes a terrible side effect called "the-paint-it-white-syndrome." I've found this afflicts mostly men, generally already known as not being as flexible as women.

You don't have to go from having a wild party to a sit-down stare-down.

One drunk at every party is kind of fun and it does give everyone something to talk about. Not that I believe being drunk all the time is beneficial, but if you understand the analogy in the spirit of harmless social antics, my hope is that you can see that colors that are attention-grabbing can be a great way to liven up things. Of course, too lively of a color becomes obnoxious, one of those downsides of drinking as well.

Just know your seating arrangement. A neglected living room may need that great bright yellow more than the already busy dining room. The den may need a more stimulating rich color than the small powder room next to it. Let a couple of the colors have the attention and let the rest of the party enjoy the spectacle.

If you learn to *see* color and you understand what you are seeing, the pot of gold at the end of the rainbow can transform your life and allow you to experience a world of beauty through color.

Afterword

As mentioned in my introduction, it wouldn't be a book about color without color treats. I'd like to invite you to check out my website section, www.devinecolor.com/colorpeeks, where you will be able to see color relationships in all their natural glory. Endless variations and combinations of color are available to our eyes and I've included many of my favorites on the site. You'll be able to see how yellow and purple work together, combined with perhaps orange, blue, or green.

I selected the images for their unusually satisfying combination of colors, many of them abstract, not definable. The pictures are a collection of photographs taken by Lake Oswego photographer Meredith Schatz, who has a remarkable talent for finding colors in the most unexpected places in the great Northwest. I've also included a personal collection of photos that reflect the beauty of nature ranging from my homeland of Puerto Rico to my own backyard.

I hope that by using the information that you will have gleaned from these pages, you will be more confident, more experimental, and more relaxed with your choices in your own home. I would love to hear your feedback so please email any reviews, comments, or concerns to askgretchen@devinecolor.com.